ONCE UPON
A TOON

For Kieran.
A Newcastle United fan.
A great man.

ONCE UPON A TOON

18 YEARS INSIDE NEWCASTLE UNITED

Best Wishes,
Paul Ferris

PAUL FERRIS

BLOOMSBURY SPORT
LONDON · OXFORD · NEW YORK · NEW DELHI · SYDNEY

BLOOMSBURY SPORT
Bloomsbury Publishing Plc
50 Bedford Square, London, WC1B 3DP, UK
Bloomsbury Publishing Ireland Limited,
29 Earlsfort Terrace, Dublin 2, D02 AY28, Ireland

BLOOMSBURY, BLOOMSBURY SPORT and the Diana logo are trademarks of
Bloomsbury Publishing Plc

First published in Great Britain 2025

Copyright © Paul Ferris, 2025

Inside photographs © Getty Images

Paul Ferris has asserted his right under the Copyright, Designs and Patents Act, 1988,
to be identified as Author of this work

All rights reserved. No part of this publication may be: i) reproduced or transmitted in
any form, electronic or mechanical, including photocopying, recording or by means of
any information storage or retrieval system without prior permission in writing from the
publishers; or ii) used or reproduced in any way for the training, development or operation
of artificial intelligence (AI) technologies, including generative AI technologies. The rights
holders expressly reserve this publication from the text and data mining exception as per
Article 4(3) of the Digital Single Market Directive (EU) 2019/790

A catalogue record for this book is available from the British Library

Library of Congress Cataloguing-in-Publication data has been applied for

ISBN: HB: 978-1-3994-2011-2; eBook: 978-1-3994 -2009-9

2 4 6 8 10 9 7 5 3 1

Typeset by D.R.INK in Adobe Garamond Pro

Printed and bound in Great Britain by Clays Ltd, Elcograf S.p.A.

To find out more about our authors and books visit www.bloomsbury.com and sign up for
our newsletters

For product safety, related questions contact productsafety@bloomsbury.com

Contents

Foreword by Alan Shearer	IX
Prologue	XV
'Just get undressed for me . . .'	1
Magnificent dilapidation	4
'What does your wife do for a living?'	5
Ted and Vi	8
My (dis)continued education	8
Benwell Bill	11
Preseason training: cheating, a bin liner and a slap	15
'So Far Away'	19
The secret pool	23
David McCreery's hair	25
The Kevin Keegan effect: 1982–84	29
A plastic pitch and a shopping trip	29
Superman, the squadron leader, and a very angry Irishman	33
The wisdom of Arthur	37
Meeting an idol	40
The man in the white coat	44
'Did we score that one?'	46
'You probably don't remember me . . .'	49
The Gallowgate roar	51
Jack Charlton, a death threat and a missing gun	53
George Reilly wins a fight	55
Once Upon a Time in America	58
'Is Geraldine there?'	61
The character and kindness of 'Zico'	65
Joe Harvey's knees	66
'Is that Spandau Ballet?'	69

Shearer – a Newcastle United Legend	72
'Divvent touch the soup . . .'	74
One minute you're Steve McQueen . . .	76
Slipping out of the back door	79
Walking through the front door	81
'I thought you drove an Aston Martin?'	84
The Kevin Keegan effect – 1992–97	86
'She *is* looking at him!'	87
The Young Ones	90
'D'you wanna go for a drink?'	91
A Newcastle United family	93
The bell rings for round one	94
The weigh-in, scissors and a trip to the post office	97
Maiden Castle	100
Poulet à la compote, a strapping and a grumpy Belgian	101
A waste of time . . .	105
Gazza and a missing passport	108
Substance behind the style	111
The versatility and timekeeping of Faustino Asprilla	112
The smiling assassin	115
The Fulwell End is always full . . .	116
Shear brilliance	119
An unhappy manager, a Christmas do and a pink tutu	120
The pride of Cookstown	124
An enthusiastic student	125
A Yorkshire terrier	128
A Psycho mummy	129
Talking to Bruce Fucking Springsteen	132
The General	134
A fan in the treatment room	135
'I Put a Spell on You'	140
A Cup final – and a prized possession	143

El Gordo and El Gordito	145
'They don't eat the green sweets . . .'	148
Ruining Gazza's diet	151
'There's always someone with a bigger boat!'	155
A book signing	158
'Wait until you hear him sing!'	160
A stray testicle, a tough Geordie and a convention of nuns	163
A familiar voice and a kind gesture	167
Ruining Bobby Robson's training session	169
'You've changed . . .'	172
The Pied Piper of the Left Bank	174
A Man for All Seasons	176
Elevation	177
Alan Shearer or Elliot Lee?	179
Bono's glasses	180
The king of Barcelona	183
A dedicated superstar	184
An iconic celebration	185
The humble winner	187
'It's only a bit of bloody wind . . .'	188
'What's my name?'	190
One player, two managers	193
A date with a masseur	196
40	198
The Master Chronicler	202
'Are ye not the trainer for N'castle, like?'	203
'What will happen to Gareth?'	205
'Can I finish my song?'	206
It was over. I just didn't know it . . .	208
A final pilgrimage	210
'Run for Home'	214
Once upon a toon . . .	215
Acknowledgements	216

Alan Shearer strikes a familiar pose, shooting for goal during the UEFA Cup match v FC Zurich in November 1999.

Standing alongside Alan Shearer before his first game as a manager v Chelsea in April 2009. It was a proud moment for me, returning to Newcastle United for the third time.

Foreword
by Alan Shearer

This is the third book by Paul Ferris and this is the third foreword from me. I am familiar with hat-tricks.

I know *Once Upon a Toon* will be as successful and is as insightful as Paul's two previous books, *The Boy on the Shed* and *The Magic in the Tin*.

This is pure football compared to those two, with many anecdotes from the weird world of professional football and Newcastle United. I'd forgotten about those nuns in Colorado!

It will soon be 30 years since I first met Paul Ferris in his capacity as Newcastle United's physiotherapist, and we have been firm friends and colleagues ever since. His has been an extraordinary career, first as a Newcastle player, then as a physio, then as a barrister, an entrepreneur and now as a writer – the award-winning *The Boy on the Shed* is currently being turned into a movie.

His life, as detailed in that book and in *The Magic in the Tin*, revealed another side to him, particularly his experiences dealing with prostate cancer in the latter book. That was tough going, but 'Ferra', as I and so many inside Newcastle know him, made it funny.

That's the man I first met in 1996 when I was signing for Newcastle from Blackburn Rovers – a serious professional, a funny bloke – and it comes across in these pages as well.

There are some poignant memories in here of great friends of ours, such as Gary Speed. But mainly this is a book packed with vivid tales of Newcastle United life – from the inside. It will entertain every single fan – whether it's George Reilly's chin, Jack Charlton's gun or the 'velly volatile' Faustino Asprilla, you'll be laughing your way through story after story. Together it all conveys what the club and football brought to Paul, and he to Newcastle United.

As someone once said – almost – *you'll love it.*

Alan Shearer

FOREWORD

Not even a cage can spoil the thrill of promotion. Newcastle fans behind the St James' Park security fences in May 1984.

The Gallowgate Choir in 1981. Conductor at the ready.

Anyone for beans on toast? It was all the rage in 1984. Haircuts got worse as the decade progressed. Well, mine certainly did anyway.

Prologue

I was 10 years old when I played for Newcastle United for the first time. It was in 1976, a couple of months after I'd sat glued to the television and watched Dennis Tueart break Kieran Moran's heart. Tueart's bicycle kick goal for Manchester City was worthy of winning any Cup final – and it did just that to defeat Kieran's beloved Newcastle United. Kieran informed me the goal was all the more painful because Tueart was a Geordie by birth, had been rejected by Newcastle United, and had made his name playing for bitter rivals Sunderland. That all meant nothing to me. I thought about asking what 'Geordie' meant, but, in truth, I didn't really care. I was far too busy obsessing over Kevin Keegan. All the boys at my school in Lisburn, Northern Ireland, were either Liverpool fans, hence my Kevin Keegan fixation, or Manchester United fans, courtesy of George Best.

My brother-in-law Kieran was the first Newcastle United fan I ever met. In the spring of 1976, my school organised a five-a-side competition. By the time I'd got my Liverpool team together, our team name had already been taken. We quickly switched to Manchester United, but that too was reserved. So distressed were we that we couldn't even think of another team any of us wanted to be. So we didn't register. I was telling Kieran of my dilemma over dinner. Thirty minutes later, I knew all about Hughie Gallacher, Jackie Milburn and Malcolm Macdonald. I learned that Newcastle was a city in the far north-east of England, and that St James' Park, the home of Newcastle United, was a Citadel, perched at the very heart of it. He knew so much, and spoke with such passion, that I thought he must have been a regular visitor. In fact, he'd never been. He longed to go, though.

The following day, spurred on by Kieran's devotion, I registered my team as Newcastle United. Two days later, I captained us to glory over Liverpool in the final. Then, the following day, I forgot all about Newcastle United. Instead, I was Kevin Keegan again, running rings around my friends in the park.

In the intervening years, until my arrival at Newcastle United in 1981, aged 16, I never gave Newcastle or its football team much of a thought. I knew about Lindisfarne's 'Run for Home', through Kieran. I was familiar with Sting and the Police. Dire Straits' *Making Movies* was the first album I bought. I loved the lyrics of 'Run for Home'. Back then they conjured images of the streets of my home in Ireland, not those of Alan Hull's Newcastle Upon Tyne, in faraway England. Apart from conversations with Kieran about the odd result here and there, Newcastle United football club was not on my horizon. At 14, I signed schoolboy forms for Bolton Wanderers, with the guarantee of a two-year apprenticeship when I reached 16. That was my footballing destiny, until one day it wasn't. In the weeks prior to the commencement of my apprenticeship, the entire footballing staff of Bolton Wanderers were sacked. All of them. From the manager right down to the youth development officer who dealt with the new apprentices. From that moment, I never heard another word from Bolton Wanderers. At 16, my footballing life was mapped out in front of me, then someone stole the map.

I fretted for a day or two, then realised I might be able to stay at home with my family after all, and I was content with that state of affairs. My bliss didn't last. Within weeks, other football clubs were contacting my parents. Tottenham Hotspur was a possibility, before there was solid interest from two other 'big' clubs. Trials at Everton and Newcastle United were hastily arranged. I travelled to Everton and hated every minute of my experience. I spent a week in Newcastle. I wouldn't say I loved it, but I liked the people around the club. The boys I met were warm and welcoming. I'd only just got home from my Newcastle trial when offers came from both clubs. There were two or three other clubs also expressing an interest. My preference was still to stay at home. It quickly became apparent that just wasn't going to

PROLOGUE

Scoring a goal for Newcastle United at the Gallowgate End, against Bradford City in 1984. What I hoped would be the first of many, proved to be the only one.

be an option. I talked to several of my family, I talked to my teachers, I talked to my boys' club managers, and I talked to Kieran. After that talk, I decided that Newcastle United was the club for me, and that the city of Newcastle was to be my home for the next two years at least. My parents were happy, my teachers delighted, my boys club managers thrilled. My Newcastle United-loving brother-in-law was ecstatic. It is undoubtedly because of the sterling job Kieran Moran did back then, in selling his club to me, that I've lived for over four decades in Newcastle. My two years at Newcastle United, extended to five years as a player from 1981 to 1986, thirteen years as a physiotherapist from 1993 to 2006, and a short stint as part of Alan Shearer's management team in 2009. It was quite the journey. Throughout it, I developed my own love and devotion to an amazing city, its generous people and its unique football club. I met and worked with incredible individuals. I shared moments that were amazing, sometimes unbelievable.

I lived and breathed the club for 18 years of my life. I may have left Newcastle United for the final time in 2009, but the club has never left me. Memories of times good and bad remain etched on my brain. I am forever asked to recount stories from my time inside

Newcastle United. I've told some of them so many times they have become a part of me. I never once, however, thought about writing about my specific experiences from within the club. That all changed over a coffee with a friend. Playwright Ed Waugh, a Newcastle United fanatic, spent an evening telling me that I should commit my recollections to print. Initially, I wasn't convinced, but the more he spoke, the more I warmed to the idea. What follows is a direct result of that conversation. I recognised that not only was there was some merit in placing on record some of the lighter, funnier and peculiar moments of life behind the scenes at a professional football club, but that it would hopefully lead to a very entertaining book.

All the stories you will read are true and are recounted as best as I can remember them. Most are first-hand experiences, unique to me and my interactions with players, managers and staff members. In most instances, I reveal the names of the individuals involved. For others, it is necessary to protect the anonymity of the protagonists in order not to subject them to ridicule or embarrassment. The stories lose none of their potency or humour as a result. *Once Upon a Toon* can be read chronologically, but can also be delved into at any point. Each tale can be enjoyed individually.

I hope you enjoy immersing yourself in some of the funniest, weirdest and most wonderful moments of my 18-year association with Newcastle United. I certainly enjoyed revisiting my experiences within professional football. I didn't fully appreciate it back then, but I know now that those years were undoubtedly some of the best of my life. I regard it as a great privilege to share my memories of those special times with you.

Paul Ferris

PROLOGUE

Back in the big league. Photoshoot in front of an empty Gallowgate End, on the eve of Newcastle United's return to the first division for the 1984/85 season.

An open training session in August 2006. My final day as a physiotherapist before leaving for Bar School.

A bulging Gallowgate End watches Kevin Keegan's debut v QPR, in 1982. An unforgettable day for all of us who had the privilege of being there.

ONCE UPON A TOON

From the pit to the pitch. Local hero, and former coal miner, Alan Shoulder celebrates his goal v Cambridge United in 1981. We will never see his like again...

'Just get undressed for me...'

My 18-year association with Newcastle United began in late October 1981. When I celebrated my sixteenth birthday four months previously, I had no idea that life as I knew it was about to change forever in a matter of a few short months. To say I was naïve at 16 would be an enormous insult to naïve people all over the world. Naïve was only part of who I was when I left my home in Northern Ireland to chase my dream of becoming a football star. I was frightened, I was lonely, I was homesick, and I was out of my comfort zone. I was also determined to do well, not just for myself but for my family back home who had hopes and dreams for me every bit as big as the ones I had for myself. I was keen to learn, I was determined to succeed, and I was eager to please. It was that attitude I brought with me to my medical examination, which formed a necessary part of my first few days as an apprentice professional footballer.

The club physio drove me to the private clinic in Jesmond, an upmarket suburb of the strange new city that was now my home. Growing up in a council estate in Lisburn, Northern Ireland, I wasn't even aware such places existed, so I was naturally a little apprehensive as we made our way through the plush reception and on towards the radiology department. The physio left me in the waiting room while he went off in search of coffee. I flicked through some magazines showing off the houses and cars I would soon be buying once I'd made my fortune as a footballer. For now, I'd have to settle for the attic room of someone else's house in my new city. I was disturbed by a gentle hand on my shoulder. A tall dark-haired thirty-something woman smiled at me as I placed my magazine on the table.

'Paul Ferris? If you follow me, I'll get your scans done now.'

I looked left and right, but there was no sign of the physio. I don't know why, but I'd just presumed he would come with me and guide me through the process. I'd only just met him a couple of days previously, but at least he was a familiar face in this strange sterile place. He was nowhere to be seen. She was already on the hoof, and heading towards the double doors to the right of the plant-laden reception.

'Should I wait for the physio so he can come in with me?'

She didn't break stride or turn around.

'That won't be necessary. He won't fit into the scanner with you anyway.'

She laughed at her own one-liner and held the door open.

I could see my fear reflected in her glasses.

She saw my fear through the same lens.

'There really is nothing to worry about. We'll be all done very quickly. It's a totally painless experience. All you have to do is lie still and I'll do the rest. The MRI will give us images of your hips, knees and ankles. At your age, I doubt we'll find anything to concern us.'

Comforted by her response, I followed her into the pristine room. The huge scanner dominated half of it. My comfort didn't last long.

'If you'd pop behind the screen there, just get undressed for me and remove any jewellery you might be wearing. I'll get things set up here. Just pop back out when you're ready.'

Just get undressed for me?

I'm not sure what I was expecting from my new career as a footballer, but I hadn't expected to be parading my naked 16-year-old body in front of a stranger less than a week after I'd been sitting in a classroom back home in Ireland. I trudged behind the screen with all the enthusiasm of a condemned man approaching the gallows. I took a few deep breaths and removed all of my clothes. Then I froze. I stood behind that screen, hoping that if I stayed long enough, she might forget I was there in the first place.

'Everything OK back there?'

My voice cracked as I answered.

'Yes, all good.'

I sounded more six than sixteen. I could feel the first trickle of sweat rolling from my forehead. My armpits and palms were moist. I could hold it off no longer. I took a final deep breath. I begged my mother back home in Ireland to give me strength. Then I stepped out completely naked, with all of the fake confidence I could muster, into this alien world I now found myself in. Her high-pitched scream startled me. I'll never forget the look on her face. That poor radiographer. Her eyes locked in on my genitals as they proudly marched towards her. Her arm was raised and her finger was pointing at the screen behind my head. She raised her other arm to her face. Her hand sent her glasses spinning into the air as she covered her eyes from the horror of the milky-white boy exposing himself in front of her.

'No! No! No! There's a gown hanging on the screen behind you!'

Her finger was wagging furiously as she crouched to pick up her glasses. Her face was inches from my exposed bits. It took me a moment to realise the error of my ways, then I quickly scampered back behind the screen before her glasses had found their way back on to her violated eyes. She composed herself.

'Just come out when you have your gown on.'

I stayed there for ages, searching for a hole in the floor to crawl into and beseeching my absent mother to give me strength. No hole or mother came to my rescue. I pulled the gown over my shoulders and tied the ties. I was more than a little confused by the design, but I was in such a state of panic and embarrassment that I just wanted the day to be over. I breathed in, held my breath, and then breathed slowly out again. Then I stepped back out from behind the screen.

Since that incident, over 40 years ago now, I often try to put myself in her position. That poor unsuspecting radiographer. How must she have felt when she looked up at that moment to see the boy who'd just exposed himself step out once more from behind the screen with his gown fastened the wrong way round? The ties that were supposed to be at the back were fastened at the front. The gown didn't join in the middle. For the second time that day, her hand scrambled for her eyes, while all the while I stood there frozen, with my genitals poking out of my gown and on display once more.

Looking back, I blame naivety, nerves and my eagerness to please. I still possess the desire to please even to this day, especially when I find myself in unfamiliar environments with new people. Thankfully, that day in the private hospital in Jesmond is the only time my desire to please has led me down a path to indecent exposure.

Magnificent dilapidation

The St James' Park of 1981 was quite the sight for a young boy from Northern Ireland. I'd been to Windsor Park in Belfast. I'd visited Burnden Park, Bolton, Goodison Park, Everton, and Old Trafford, Manchester. All brilliant old stadiums bursting with character. All integral to the communities that surrounded them. I'd been informed many times before my arrival in Newcastle that St James' Park was different to other stadiums because it was actually in the city.

As I walked up the hill from Central Station, I realised that all the descriptions placing St James' in the city centre were wrong. When I caught sight of it glistening in the autumn sunshine, I felt its presence in my gut. The old main stand and the myriad of steps leading to the Gallowgate End *towered* above the city landscape. St James' Park wasn't just in the city, it was *on* the city. The stadium sat majestically perched like an old medieval castle. I bounced up the hill and in through the entrance of the Main Stand with Newcastle United emblazoned in giant letters along its length. Inside was all darkness and wood panelling. It spoke of another time. I made my way down the home tunnel and felt my heart pounding with excitement as I walked out into the empty stadium. I strolled to the centre circle.

That October day was eerily quiet. The Main Stand, built in the Edwardian era, dominated everything else around it. The East Stand, built in the 1970s, sat proudly opposite. At either end were the Gallowgate and Leazes, both uncovered. The Gallowgate End was a giant endless row of terraces with a huge scoreboard above it. The Leazes End was a sorry rump of terracing with a bare wall behind it. Rows of paddocks and benches sat below the Main Stand and the East Stand. There was an unusual smell about the place too. Not unpleasant, but not pleasant either. I later found out that it was the smell of the hops wafting across the road from the Scottish and Newcastle Brewery opposite. The stadium was a reflection of the city itself in the early '80s. It had clearly once been majestic; it had experienced its fair share of glory days. But in 1981, the city of Newcastle was in a state of depression and decline. The old industries were gone, or on their way out, with nothing seemingly on the horizon to stem the rising tide of unemployment and sense of hopelessness. The giant stadium that dominated it was still something to behold, though, even if it was in dire need of investment and modernisation.

In October 1981, when I joined the club, the once mighty St James' Park was in a state of magnificent dilapidation. Something needed to change. Thankfully, a revolution was just around the corner.

'What does your wife do for a living?'

I was head boy at St Patrick's Secondary School in Lisburn before my education was abruptly halted by my move to Newcastle United. The school had no sixth form, hence the head boy role being given to a 16-year-old. I'd failed my eleven-plus, which had more to do with its timing coinciding with our home being petrol bombed in a sectarian attack than any lack of academic ability. It was very apparent to the teaching staff at St Patrick's that I was a bright boy, and my exam results throughout my time at school provided confirmation. So much so, that by the time Newcastle United came calling, I was a head boy who was intending to leave school the following summer to commence my A levels at Rathmore Grammar School, just outside the town. From there, my ambition was to read Law at Queen's University Belfast. The best laid plans . . .

In spite of my previous achievements at school, and indeed of having the intention of continuing my education alongside my football career at Newcastle United, it didn't take long for me to lose my confidence in my academic prowess soon after my arrival at the club. Within a matter of weeks I'd forgotten I was ever clever at school and instead convinced myself I was anything but. The reasons for my sudden belief that not only was I stupid, but I might very well be the most stupid apprentice professional footballer currently on the books at Newcastle United, were threefold. Firstly, I have been in possession of an irrational insecurity all of my life. I continue to fight against it even to this day, and in those early days away from home and family it was raging hard. Secondly, my new teammates never missed an opportunity to remind me every day just how thick and how stupid I was – *thick Paddy... dopey Irish... Have you heard the one about Pat and Mick?... An Englishman, Irishman, and Scotsman . . .* – and on and on it would go. Thirdly, when I'd meet people away from the football club, the conversation would often go something along these lines:

'What do you do for a living?'
'Oh, I'm a footballer.'
'You must be a bit thick, then. Are you Irish as well?'
'Yes, I'm Irish too.'
'Wow. You must be doubly thick.'

The combination of all of the above ensured that I quickly forgot all about only recently being head boy and my aspirations to study law. Instead, I wandered around the city of Newcastle for months convincing myself I was absolutely the thickest person in Thickville. Until one day I was jogging behind Jeff Clarke, one of the obviously brighter senior players. After his playing career ended, he would go off to university and become a well-respected physiotherapist. Jeff was jogging alongside one of the other first-team players – one of the very people who used to remind me every time we interacted just how thick the Irish were. We were trotting along and Jeff's jogging partner was chatting along too.

'Hey, Jeff. I've been meaning to ask. What does your missus do for a living?'

Jeff replied instantly, without breaking stride.

'She's an estate agent.'

His inquisitor took some time to digest this information before delivering his considered response.

'Fuck me. You lucky bastard. That's you sorted for your holidays, then, isn't it!'

Jeff turned to me and smiled. I laughed out loud. Jeff's inquisitor was oblivious.

The same player was part of a card school on away trips. I'd started travelling with the first team within months of my arrival. I was still only 16 and sitting on the adjacent table one day when he threw his cards onto the table.

'That's me done. I'm out.'

The other three players tried to convince him to continue and not to ruin their game. He had the perfect retort to get them off his case.

'Listen, I've got no colossal left!'

They burst out laughing. He was completely bemused. The most senior of them shouted over to me.

'Hey Paul. D' you wanna to tell him or shall I?'

I took great pleasure in doing so.

'I think the word you're looking for is *collateral*.'

He was having none of it.

'What? What's *collateral*?'

I was having fun.

'The thing you have none of.'

He shook his head.

'*Collateral* means money? I had no idea.'

I sat back in my chair. Maybe I wasn't so thick after all.

Ted and Vi

Moving to another country when still but a boy is a life-shattering event. It certainly felt that way to me when I left Northern Ireland for my new life in England. The sudden separation from all the people I knew and loved was a brutal wrench. It still makes me shudder today when I think of how bereft I felt during my early days in Newcastle. For a long time after my arrival, I felt lost and alone. That all changed the day I moved into my lodgings with Ted and Vi Hughes in Gosforth. These kind-hearted people, still reeling from the loss of their precious daughter Maureen, showered me with a love and kindness that I didn't fully appreciate at the time, but which I've never forgotten. Ted was engaging, gregarious and interested in my football and my family. Vi was warm, laughed loud and long, and a phenomenal cook. They welcomed me into their family like I was one of their own. I regret I never told them just what that meant to me.

My (dis)continued education

When Newcastle United came knocking on my door when I was 16, it would be fair to say that I was less than enthusiastic about being yanked from my home, my family and my girlfriend, Geraldine. In fact, I explored every possible avenue to try to convince the adults making the life-changing decisions about my future that I should stay at home for just a little while longer. My final gambit was to persuade my parents and my teachers that my move to England should be postponed at least until after I'd sat my O levels. My teachers were predicting great things for me in those upcoming exams and I was doing quite well convincing everyone that this was obviously the best course of action for all concerned. Then Brian Watson, Newcastle

United's youth development officer, promised my parents that I could continue my education alongside my apprenticeship as a footballer. That was enough to seal my fate, and I was gone. He kept his promise too . . . well, sort of.

I was expecting to be enrolled in college to complete my O levels. Instead, I joined the other, often very reluctant, apprentice professionals, on a course at Newcastle College. It all ended in chaos. Even to this day, I'm not sure what the point of that course was. I am sure that the diploma we received for completing it was an absolute waste of the paper it was printed on. Ironically, five years later, after my career had ended all too prematurely, I was forced to return to Newcastle College, to complete the education I'd been promised at 16, in order to start my journey to university and my physiotherapy career.

Perhaps it says something about the expectations society had for working-class kids in the 1980s that the subjects we studied every Thursday included brick laying, arc welding, wall papering, wiring electricity sockets, and learning about the social deprivation of working-class, inner-city areas. The arc welding studies were cancelled after the third week because our centre-forward thought it was a good idea to chase the rest of us around the room with his blowtorch. The fact that he was obviously drunk at the time injected considerable jeopardy.

As part of our course, we were also taken on a team bonding trip to the Lake District. It, too, ended in farce. In one counselling exercise we were invited to sit in a circle on the floor and encouraged to offer criticisms of one another without fear or concern for hurting the recipient's feelings. The target of the criticism was then offered the opportunity to respond. Our drunken centre-forward, he of the blowtorch, decided I would be his target. He pointed to me.

'Well . . . like . . . well . . . like . . . like . . . like . . . he . . . like . . . he like . . . he like . . . he . . . he . . . he like . . . he thinks he's really clever and all that . . . and like . . . and he like . . . he thinks he's better than the rest of us . . . like and all that like.'

I was taken aback. Encouraged to respond, I did so calmly. On reflection, maybe I should've chosen my words more carefully.

'Well, I'm certainly cleverer than you. You can't even speak properly, you thick bastard.'

All hell broke loose. I'm not sure who stepped across his path as he lunged towards me, but I'm very grateful he did. It took about 30 minutes to calm down our centre-forward. I don't think that discussion played out quite how the counsellor had envisaged, and the session was aborted.

I learned a valuable lesson that day: that I had a particularly sharp tongue and that it could land me in trouble. I've curbed the urge to use it as I have got older and wiser. I know now that it's not always appropriate to blurt out the very first thing that comes into my head when I'm challenged. Having said that, he was a thick bastard.

The whole course came crashing down around us on one memorable afternoon at the Rye Hill campus at Newcastle College. Our room overlooked Cruddas Park, a particularly neglected and run-down area of the city. There were nine of us left of the twelve who had commenced the course. The self-important sociology lecturer, who'd been brought in especially for the occasion, was staring moodily out of the window as he talked to the Cruddas Park housing estate beyond it. The good people of Cruddas Park were probably paying more attention to the wisdom he was imparting than most of our group. I was at the front of the room with Chris Hedworth, the only other apprentice who had an interest in anything remotely resembling academia and learning. My good friend John Carver was chewing pens and throwing paper, with the rest of the group, at the back of the class. Then it all kicked off. The bearded academic tapped the window as he delivered the final flourish to his underwhelming lecture.

'Social deprivation is the scourge of our time. It's a blight on our children and obliterates their chances in life. Inequality in our country is at an all-time high. It'll only get worse if we don't act now.'

He jabbed his accusing finger hard on the window to emphasise his anger at the unfairness of it all.

'I mean look down there. Look at Cruddas Park. It's little more than a slum. A filthy neglected slum. What chance does any poor child have if they are brought up in that environment? None. None whatsoever. It needs to be demolished. It needs to be razed to the ground –'

'Ho!'

I turned to see where the noise was coming from. John was on his feet. Both hands were in the air.

'Ho, man! I fucking live there, you cheeky bastard! I fucking live there!'

With that, our lecture was over and our course was ended. My promised education was nothing more than a ruse to get me to Newcastle as soon as possible. We all graduated and got our diplomas in pointlessness. I returned home for the holidays that summer. I watched as my former classmates completed their O levels, and was so envious. I did know how to wire a plug and hang wallpaper, though. I bet they didn't. I'd also made my debut for Newcastle United. That was a pretty good consolation.

Benwell Bill

The Newcastle United I joined in the early '80s operated on an entirely different level to the ultra-professional multimillion pound business it is today. That's true of the whole of football. The creation of the Premier League, Sky TV and the multibillionaires investing in several of our elite clubs has changed the face of football. While the mind-boggling riches don't always filter their way down the pyramid as they should, there is little doubt that, even down to grassroots level, the game has changed forever and for the better.

It was 2009 when I departed from Newcastle United for the third and final time. Yet even then, when it was trapped in the financial straitjacket of the Mike Ashley era, it operated in another universe to how it did in the '80s. The takeover in 2021 all but guarantees that the club is destined to become one of the giants of world football over the coming decade and beyond. The stadium will be redeveloped or relocated. The capacity will increase to service the insatiable demand of the many frustrated thousands currently on the waiting list. The training facility at Longbenton will be reimagined or relocated. It currently lags far behind those of most of the Premier League. The overhaul will be as high on the list of priorities for an upgrade as the playing staff itself. Yet staggeringly, decidedly average as it is, that training facility is a jaw-dropping improvement on the old Benwell Training Ground that was home to the club in the '80s. Great players like Kevin Keegan, Terry McDermott, Peter Beardsley and Chris Waddle reported for their daily work to a facility that wouldn't have met the standards of a local council recreation complex. The brilliant skills of Paul Gascoigne were honed in the often long grass of the three training pitches, or on the bone-hard rubber surface of the frequently freezing indoor hangar. My own promising career came to a premature end when my studs became tangled in that long grass. My mangled left knee never recovered from the damage inflicted upon it as my body twisted one way and my knee rotated in the opposite direction.

The changing rooms at Benwell were housed in a one-storey brick building. The first team dressing room was to the right as you walked through the front door. The tiny boot room was there, too. To the left was the reserve team dressing room. Straight ahead was a communal sitting area, with the manager's office to be found on the left side, halfway into the room. At the far end, doors faced you on the left and on the right. The one to the left opened into a cupboard room, into which the coaches squeezed themselves, and beyond their cramped space was the physio room. We may have had a physio room, but for some of my time as a player, we had no physio. It was only after a delegation of senior players approached Jack Charlton in the mid '80s to complain about the medical department – or should I say the absence of one? – that this staggering lack of care for player welfare was addressed. Until then, Newcastle United footballers had less access to a qualified physiotherapist than a Sunday league player visiting his local hospital.

Derek Wright arrived and everything changed for the better. The training ground operated with a full-time staff consisting of a manager,

The scoreboard in 1982.

two coaches and a physio. They were supported by a part-time chief scout, part-time coaches at the weekends and a Church of England vicar, who appeared, miraculously, every Friday afternoon.

There was one other member of staff who was an ever-present fixture at Benwell. Behind the door to the right, at the far end of the communal area, was a narrow passage that led to the two gigantic dryers in the laundry room. There were no washing machines in there, just dryers. When I was a 16-year-old apprentice, it was a free-for-all in the laundry room to establish who could find the least smelly kit to wear in the afternoon. This was usually after it had been worn by someone else that morning. I can still smell the stench from the stiff socks to this day. I got ringworm within weeks of arriving at the club from wearing someone else's filthy training kit.

The other member of staff didn't reside in the laundry room. He lived in the narrow passageway. When I say lived, he was a pleasant presence first thing in the morning, and equally as jovial in the afternoons. He stood behind a narrow white counter and was ever ready to serve anyone who entered his kingdom. His name was Bill, and he made the tea. Nothing else, just the tea. When I think of the restaurant quality breakfasts and lunches I became accustomed to when I returned to Newcastle United in the '90s, it seems both quaint and staggering that the club who signed Kevin Keegan, and produced Chris Waddle, Peter Beardsley and Paul Gascoigne, offered nothing but a cup of tea before and after a training session to fuel, refuel and replenish its biggest assets.

What a cup of tea it was, though! I was reared in an Irish household, where a pot of tea was always on the stove. When it reached the cup, it was always thick and strong. It was tea, how tea should be. So was Bill's. Bill's tea was a work of art. Always piping hot and always very strong. He took real pride in it. Anyone who ventured into that passageway was greeted the same way every day.

'Cup of tea, sir?'

He looked 85 years old, though I suspect he may have been 20 years younger than that. His face was thin and veiny, his hair was a wisp and nothing more. His eyes were yellow and matched by his three surviving teeth. His gnarled and trembling hands fascinated and saddened me, as they struggled to hold the huge teapot over the plastic cups while he filled them with his nectar. More often than not, he couldn't manage to hold the pot still for long enough and he'd pour his tea over his pristine counter. He'd admonish himself and apologise profusely. It was then that you could really smell the previous night's excesses on his laboured breath.

'Oh dear. So sorry about that, sir. I'll get you a fresh one in a jiffy.'

I don't know if any of the other players ever stopped to talk to Bill. I'm sure they must have. I hope they did. As a lonely 16-year-old boy, I spoke with him often. It all started when I complimented him on the quality of his tea. He asked about my mother and my family, and I was all too glad to tell him about both. I asked about his life before he became the tea maker to the stars. I discovered where he'd perfected his impeccable manners. He'd spent a life in service as the maître d' at prestigious hotels in London. He'd worked at the Ritz – or Claridge's, I can't remember which – but his eyes came alive when he regaled me with tales of his glory days. His glory days came to an end after alcohol tightened its grip. He lost his job, his home and his wife, and now he was an old man who made tea for companionship. I loved my chats with him and I looked forward to them every day. Until one day he wasn't there. No one was. There was no tea. And there was concern.

Enquiries were made. He was alive – and normal service was resumed the following day. Bill was back! He had some new friends with him, though. One was a huge graze down the side of his face, and the other was the best black eye I've ever seen this side of a boxing ring. He was happy to share his war story with me. He'd been out the night before last and had three or four too many. He staggered his usual route home along Gosforth High Street – and woke up the following morning lying at the bottom of the manhole he'd walked straight into the night before. By the time the confused workmen had fished him out and he was given the all-clear at the hospital, he was too late for work. I was crying with laughter by the time he'd revealed the details of his missing day. So was he. He was back every day after that. Until the day he wasn't.

Thank you, Bill. You helped a lonely boy settle in a new land. You did your family proud. You were a gentleman, sir.

Preseason training: cheating, a bin liner and a slap

I wasn't sure what to expect from my first preseason in the summer of 1982. I knew it was going to be hard. I knew it was going to be attritional. I knew it was going to hurt. I knew all of that because the other players never tired of telling me how awful it was going to be. In modern-day football, preseason is just a continuum of the season before. The summer break is very short and the highly tuned athletes spend their time exercising their way through their holiday. That was not the case in 1982. Back then, we had a six-week break.

I spent that first summer eating my way through as much chocolate as I could. When I wasn't doing that, I was gorging myself on my mother's home-made pies and potato-apple bread. I didn't so much as manage a jog from the living room to the kitchen of my small family home. By the looks of some of my teammates on our first day back, I think my mother had been feeding them double portions too.

Preseason was carnage. The object was to grit your teeth and pray you came through it unscathed. In these enlightened days of sports science, strength and conditioning, and research, preseason is a cakewalk. Sessions are tailored to the individual. In 1982, it was 'one size fits all', and it was brutal. It felt as if every day commenced with a six-mile road slog in the morning, followed by an afternoon of three consecutive twelve-minute runs, or hill runs until I threw up. I have a photograph, taken by the official club photographer, of me doing just that on top of a hill next to Gateshead stadium. I'm bent double, mid boke, in the middle of a group of equally exhausted footballers, who were all expected to morph into endurance athletes in three weeks.

My memories of the long runs are excruciating. In every long torturous run I ever completed in my five years as a professional footballer, I finished last. I'd endure them, one coach after another screaming at me as I made my way along the hilly route: 'Come on, lazy . . . Not good enough . . . Put some effort in, man . . . The old men are beating you . . .' On and on it would go. I knew I wasn't lazy, I knew I was at maximum capacity, but no matter how hard I tried, I was destined to be last. Now, I know why. I was a stockily built sprinter, with thighs full of fast-twitch muscle fibres. Over a 10-metre sprint, I don't think I ever lost a race in my whole time as a footballer. It's no fluke that the players at the front of the long runs were the tall skinny midfielders who were built to run all day long. They were also the ones who lagged way behind me in the sprints. In 1982, no one had worked that out – or if they had, they weren't employed by Newcastle United.

By the third week of demoralisation and admonishment for bringing up the rear on the long runs, I devised a cunning plan to ensure that just for once, some other poor bastard could take the abuse for coming last. The plan was pretty simple and straightforward. I was going to cheat. I'd noticed, from previous slogs, that three-quarters of the way up the never-ending hill on the West Road, there was a right turn. If I took it, I could cut off a mile or maybe more of my torture. I could then simply rejoin the group again as they looped over the top of the hill and around towards our Benwell training base. I might even have time to stop for a rest as I waited for the perfect moment to join my weary travellers. I'd need to find a gap so that no one would see me emerge from the side street. Then I'd have only a few hundred metres left to hold down my spot in the middle of the field. It was a good plan.

I was 40 minutes into my daily torture and in my usual position. The coaches had been stationed along the route at their usual vantage points. They'd jumped in their communal car and headed back to Benwell to greet the skinny players, with their slow-twitch muscle fibres, as they made their triumphant return. They'd probably have time for a cup of tea from Bill before coming back out at their leisure to scold me for my latest pathetic effort. My legs were tired. My lungs were burning. I had two sweat rashes in my groin. The blisters on both my heels were burning as I passed the crematorium on my left. There were people in there in better shape than I was at that moment. I was 50 metres behind the penultimate straggler.

The turning on the right loomed large in front of me. Beyond it, up ahead, was the steepest climb of the never-ending hill. I knew it was wrong, I knew I shouldn't do it, but I did it anyway. I turned right. I was off the hill. I was on flat ground. By the time I exited the narrow street and rejoined the route again, I'd have shaved 10 minutes off my time. No one would be any the wiser. I was so relieved to be off the hill, and on flat ground, that I didn't notice the car at first. I was plodding along on my blistered feet, bloody thighs rubbing together, and smiling to myself. All the while, the black Ford Fiesta, carrying the entire coaching staff of Newcastle United, was taxiing alongside the latest cheat who'd taken the same short cut as all the other cheats who'd ever gone before him and all those who'd ever come after him. My bliss was only spoiled when the Fiesta pulled up sharply in front of my path, causing me to run straight into the passenger side door. I thought I'd been rammed by a careless driver and shook my head furiously. I stopped shaking it when the stern-faced coach climbed out. He shook his instead. Much more vigorously than I'd been shaking mine.

'There's always one. You cheating little bastard!'

He was right on both counts. I felt sick to my stomach. I thought I was going to throw up. I didn't throw up. Well, not there and then anyway. I saved that for the training ground 40 minutes later. I reported to the coaches' room after my best ever finish in the long run. I was handed a black bin liner. This was to be worn against my skin and under my training top. Then I was escorted to one of the pitches and ordered to complete three consecutive twelve-minute runs as fast as I could manage. If my lap time dropped below a certain level, I was to complete another twelve-minute run. I don't know how I managed to complete my punishment with the bin liner clinging tightly to my skin. But I did. When I'd finished, I unrolled the bottom of the bin liner. A torrent of pooled sweat gushed down my legs. My vomit followed. I never cheated on a run again.

That afternoon, I joined the rest of the group for more torture. I completed eight consecutive 400-metre runs, minus my bin liner. I was running in a team of four, alongside my hero, and recently arrived superstar, Kevin Keegan. I was determined not to be dropped by the group. On our fifth or sixth run I was flagging, breathing hard and hanging in there just in front of Kevin. My legs felt like they were about to explode and my lungs were attempting to burst out of my mouth. As we slowed to a halt for a very welcome breather, I received a good old-fashioned clip round my ear. Kevin lowered his hand and bent over as he gasped for air.

'Jesus Christ. Will you stop groaning like that when you're running. You're making me tired!'

I hadn't even noticed, but apparently with every breath I was making a moaning sound not dissimilar to a foghorn. That may have had something to do with my exertions an hour earlier.

In my first preseason I was caught cheating, sweated buckets into a bin liner and got a clip around the ear from Kevin Keegan my footballing hero. That preseason was most definitely unforgettable. Far worse than anything the senior players had warned me it would be; more hideous than I'd ever imagined it could be.

'So Far Away'

Newcastle is close to nowhere. Well, that's not entirely true. It's close to Scotland and it's also very close to the North Sea. Neither of those facts are of much use when you're sitting on a coach, on the A1 or M6, at 1 a.m. on a Thursday morning, and you know that you're getting back on that same coach on Friday afternoon for a five-hour journey to your next destination.

As a young footballer, recently yanked from the tiny province of Northern Ireland, where every place is close to every other place, I grew to hate the travelling to and from games. It wasn't too bad if you were just travelling with the reserve team every other Wednesday, or if you were a first-team regular, heading off on a Friday or a Saturday morning every other weekend. If you were an in-betweener, as I was for most of my short playing career, you were required for both journeys. The upshot was that on some weeks I felt like I spent more time on the coach than I did on the training pitch. Don't get me wrong, the coaches we travelled on weren't your standard offering. They were luxurious. Four seats per table, a toilet, a kitchen and a lounge area at the back. TV monitors throughout and a great stereo system.

I'd initially enjoyed the novelty and the luxury of my first few four-hour journeys down the A1. I felt like a proper footballer arriving at the familiar stadiums I'd only ever marvelled at on the TV. I loved skipping off the coach to howls of abuse from the home fans and back on it again for fish and chips and the long sleepy ride home. It quickly became all a bit too monotonous, though. When I'd bedded in and was a little more confident, I began providing the music tapes for our long journeys. I've always loved music and I took great pride in creating an eclectic mix of songs that was sure to appeal to someone some of the time. In the early days, my main reason for supplying the music was to ensure I wasn't subjected to four hours of German porn grunting out of the TV monitor above my head. If certain senior players were travelling, there was no choice in the matter. It was porn all the way. I'm not a prude in any way, but I've never been a fan of communal porn. I certainly wasn't at 16. Wasn't the whole point of porn to watch it in privacy? I would've much preferred *The Godfather* (Part I or II) or even *E.T.* In the early days, my mixtapes sometimes had to compete with Roy Chubby Brown cassettes. I persevered and it wasn't long before the senior players were asking me if I was bringing my latest compilation on the next trip. The music made the long journeys tolerable for me. I wasn't a card player and Trivial Pursuit hadn't yet reached our coach.

The music was my lifeline. That is, until the grumpiest coach driver in the world took a disliking to it. Bob was his name. He was Newcastle United's regular coach driver throughout the early '80s. Thickset, with slicked-back, thinning hair and a facial expression that alternated between mildly constipated and just dropped a load in his trousers. He was never pleasant, never smiled, and when he spoke, it was only to grunt or bark. He was just a grumpy old bastard. He knew he was a grumpy old bastard, and he revelled in being a grumpy old bastard. He must have, or why else would he have so brilliantly perfected the art? In all my time spent travelling on his luxury coach, I never once saw him smile, and I don't think I heard him mutter anything other than swear words and insults.

I resolved very early to avoid unnecessary interaction with Bob. Unfortunately, my love of music meant I had to speak with him to ask him to insert my cassette tapes. I initially had no inkling that my music had become a real issue for him until I was already at war. He was battling me and I didn't even realise we were both in the trenches. I'd approach him as we were driving out of the training ground or stadium. I'd politely ask him to put the cassette in the player. He wouldn't take his eyes of the road. He'd snatch it from my hand and force it through the slot in front of him. He'd turn the volume down as low as he could get away with. I'd ask him to turn it up. He'd shake his head and comply. By the time I'd reached my seat, he'd have turned it back down to barely audible. A couple of shouts from the senior players meant the volume would go back up to a level where we could actually make out which artist was singing. When the music stopped, I'd approach him, hold out my hand and he'd slap the cassette into it. I'd go back to my seat, hoping to watch *Raiders of the Lost Ark*, but most probably I'd be watching German porn (it was always German!).

That was my routine, until one night I held my hand out to retrieve my Christopher Cross compilation. Bob ejected it. I waited. Bob opened his window. I waited. Then the grumpy old bastard threw Christopher Cross out onto the A1, somewhere near Scotch Corner. That's when I realised I was in the trenches. From that day I brought Christopher Cross on every trip. I lost a few cassettes on the A1 and on the M6, but when I did, I'd ask one of the senior players to pass Bob the duplicate. He'd make sure to tell him to turn it up loud and warn him not to throw his cassette out of the window. Grumpy Bob was forced to listen to Christopher Cross on every trip for a whole season.

I was glad when we started travelling to London by train. It meant no dealings with Bob. The InterCity 125 made the journey much more pleasurable. The senior players played cards, I had my Sony Walkman. All was good. Well, not quite. All was good on the way to London. I'd listen to my music safe in the knowledge it wouldn't be ending up on the railway line. I'd watch the ever-growing pile of banknotes covering the table in front of the very competitive card school of Kevin Keegan, Terry McDermott, Mick Martin and Imre Varadi. Then halfway through the trip, they'd send me to the buffet car to fetch them some bacon toasties and tea.

The problem with the train journey was that there was always the return trip. The other problem with the train journey was that I don't remember us ever winning a game in London. The problem with losing in London and getting the train back to Newcastle was that hundreds of our disappointed and angry fans were on the same train.

I'm not sure if there was a first-class section on the 125. If there was, then I don't think we, as players, were in it. Maybe those were the days when such opulence was reserved for the club directors? I remember we had a train guard stationed outside our carriage. It was just as well. After one pretty dismal performance and heavy defeat, I was dispatched to the buffet car for the bacon toasties. I made my way past the guard to the hatch. I arrived just as six or seven Newcastle fans approached from the other direction. If they didn't recognise me, they quickly recognised my official club tracksuit. Half an hour later, with my ears still burning, I dropped the bacon toasties and tea onto the card table. Imre spoke first.

'We thought you weren't coming back. I nearly came looking for you.'

I handed him his tea.

'Just as well you didn't.'

He spilled it on his cards.

'Why's that, then?'

I pointed over my shoulder to the door and to the poor guard who was holding back a sea of angry black and white.

'Cos they said to tell you, you were shit today.'

Mick spat his tea onto the table and laughed with Kevin and Terry. I spoiled his bliss.

'They said to tell you, you were shit too, Mick.'

Kevin smiled

'What about me?'

I sat down.

'They said to tell you that you're God.'

He laughed and raised his tea towards the angry mob. They chanted: 'Keegan, Keegan' all the way back to Newcastle. I suppose the moral of the story is, don't travel on the same train as the fans if you regularly lose in London – or if you are going to travel on the train after losing in London, make sure you travel with God.

The secret pool

'Would you eat your dinner off that?'

Colin Suggett, my youth team coach, was rubbing his finger along the light switch at the entrance to the home changing room at St James' Park. I did think about asking him who would ever think to eat their dinner off a light switch, but the stern look on his face made me think better of it. It was late Friday afternoon before the big game at the weekend. I was new to my role as an apprentice footballer. Colin, who'd been a player himself, was a brilliant youth team coach by morning and a stickler for cleanliness in the afternoons. The bad news for me was that no matter how much I scrubbed, cleaned and polished, there was always a light switch, or a dark corner of a cupboard, that wasn't suitable for serving a three-course meal. The good news was that I got to spend more time in the home changing room deep in the bowels of St James' Park.

It was such a novelty for me to be in this sacred place where so many great players of the past had once dwelled. The old changing room was full of character. Individual shutters marked each player's changing space. They were a bugger to clean, though. The changing room led into an area dominated by a giant communal bath. It was round and sunken into the floor, and I had to jump down into it armed with my Brillo pads. I used them to attack the rim of stubborn scum that clung there. I would be completely knackered by the time I climbed back out. Colin never climbed down into the bath to check if I would eat my dinner off it.

The bathroom area led into a long, narrow treatment room full of rickety old beds that Hughie Gallacher must have lain on. To the right just outside the bath area was a narrow corridor that led to a tiny boot room. The current players' match-day boots hung there, gleaming from all the scrubbing and polishing we apprentices devoted to them. There was also a wall hung with boots from the past. I didn't know who they once belonged to and liked to imagine they were Jackie Milburn's or Len White's. They were certainly so old that they could have been.

The boot room held another secret from the past. In the middle of the stone floor was a small wooden trapdoor. I ignored it for my first few weeks, but then curiosity got the better of me. One day, and with the help of an equally nosey apprentice, I tried to yank it open. After a considerable amount of effort, and calling in reinforcements, we managed to pull the ancient lid away from the floor. It revealed a smelly, dark, watery hole. We were about to close the lid again when I noticed a light switch. I flicked it. Two ancient bulbs sparked into life. They revealed a staircase descending into a filthy swimming pool, about five metres long and four metres wide, and just a metre beneath the roof. A secret swimming pool under St James' Park! A spooky, stinking, slimy one – but a swimming pool, nonetheless.

As we closed the trapdoor, I had two thoughts. The first: *What a ridiculously stupid place to put a swimming pool!* The second: *Thank fuck Colin Suggett doesn't know anything about it!*

David McCreery's hair

1982 was a momentous year in my life. On 1 May I made my debut for Newcastle United – and became the youngest player ever to play for that famous institution. It was also a pivotal year in the history of the club. After finishing the 1981/82 season with a whimper, the manager, Arthur Cox, turned his attention to transforming this once great club from second division also-rans to genuine promotion challengers. When I'd made my second appearance for the club, in a 4-0 home defeat by Queens Park Rangers on 5 May, there were only 10,748 fans in the half-empty old stadium. Little did they, or we as players, know, but Arthur had a plan. And what a plan it was! As we travelled to Madeira for a preseason friendly against Maritimo, Arthur stayed behind in England to complete what was, without doubt, one of the most significant signings in the history of Newcastle United.

We were in the hotel winding down after our friendly. The coach came into the room to inform us that we'd just signed Kevin Keegan. The collective shouts of 'Fuck off!', 'No fucking way!' and 'You're taking the piss!' did nothing to dampen his enthusiasm. A few phone calls home and the room suddenly buzzed with excitement as everyone came to terms with the fact that one of the world's greatest players, a two-time Ballon d'Or winner, the current England captain, and last season's First Division top scorer, had agreed to extend his stellar career with a team that had finished ninth in the second tier of English football. It's almost impossible to convey just how seismic that moment was for Newcastle United, for the city, and for us as players. Kevin Keegan was practically a deity to me and to others of my generation.

I shared a room on that trip with Kenny Wharton. I'd just turned 17 and Kenny was 21. We sat up most of the night discussing what Kevin's arrival meant for the club. We both came to the same conclusion. We didn't have a squad worthy of such a player. Arthur had pulled off a master stroke, but it would mean nothing if he couldn't supplement Kevin's arrival with other quality players to play alongside him. We didn't have long to wait before Arthur did just that. There was a flurry of activity, and several players were shipped out to make way for upgrades in the playing staff. Of those who came in, two stood out, though one was much more high profile than the other. Both would play a massive role in our eventual promotion the following season, 1983/84.

Terry McDermott arrived from Liverpool, fresh from his trophy-laden stint there (and after a previous spell at Newcastle United). He was at the tail end of his fantastic career, but there was clearly still enough fire in his belly and miles left in his ever-running legs. The other signing, who proved to be an inspired one, was David McCreery. My fellow Ulsterman had been plying his trade with Tulsa Roughnecks in the USA. He arrived a few months after Kevin and Terry, and not long after he'd been an integral part of the Northern Ireland team who'd reached the second round of the World Cup, beating the hosts Spain in the process. I was excited by his arrival on a personal level. It would be good to hear another voice from home every day at the training ground. Even though I'd quickly found my way into the first team picture since my arrival less than a year before, I still yearned for home every day – or, I should say, every night, in the loneliness of my attic room.

The imminent arrival of David, who'd embarked on the same journey as me several years before when he'd travelled to Manchester United as a 16-year-old, was certainly something to anticipate. When he did arrive, he didn't disappoint, either on or off the pitch. Off it, he was a quietly spoken gentleman – warm, kind and approachable. Only days after his arrival, he took me for a drive with him and his wife Julie as they viewed properties in search of a new home for themselves.

On the field, McCreery was distinctive – both for his appearance and his manner of play. In the era of the mullet, he had long hair but was thinning on top. He wore his shorts pulled up a little too high, but – and this is the important point – he scampered all over the midfield barking his orders to his teammates. He was ferocious in the tackle and pinpoint with his passing. He was a ball of energy in training and on match days. He became a fan favourite and was a

DAVID MCCREERY'S HAIR

The senior players posing with the kids in 1982. Those kids would go on to win the FA Youth Cup, in 1985. The smiling boy in the middle would achieve a lot more than that.

pivotal presence in the team over the next seven years. He was the perfect holding midfield player and would fit in perfectly with the modern game's emphasis on retrieving the ball, passing, moving and retaining possession. In spite of the combative nature of his game, he never seemed to get injured. If he was on the receiving end of a heavy challenge, he'd simply bounce to his feet, shake it off, and get on with his game. I've no doubt he was a dream for the manager, Arthur Cox, who was very much from that school of thought that you don't show your opponent a hint of weakness. You play the game hard and fair. I never saw David McCreery stay down after a tackle in the whole four years I spent with him at Newcastle United. Apart from once.

It was early January 1983 and we were playing Bolton Wanderers at a packed St James' Park. I was in the home dugout as 13th man in the squad. I was either sub, or the 13th man, on many occasions that season. For a 17-year-old, that represented excellent early progress in my fledgling career. It also gave me a front row seat to the match every week. It was from that vantage point that I watched David McCreery and his young teammate, Peter Haddock, slide into a tackle from either side of the unfortunate Bolton player caught in their scissors right in front of the home dugout. There was a coming together of legs, boots and studs – and a loud crunch as all three collided at speed. The referee blew his whistle to signify a foul on the Bolton player. Then everyone got up to get on with the game. Well, not everyone. David stayed on the ground. He waved his arm in the air and then pointed to his thigh. Typically, he didn't cry out or squeal in pain. He just wanted to draw our attention to his injured leg.

My eyes followed his hand. I wished they hadn't. What they saw was a gash, more than a foot in length, stretching from David's knee and running towards his hip. Peter Haddock's stud had hit him at pace and opened his thigh as efficiently as any can opener ever opened a can of beans. For a brief moment, I could see the white bubbles of subcutaneous fat that lay under his ripped skin. I could see his thigh muscles exposed and bulging out of the gap where his skin used to be. Then the blood came, gushing all over the muscles and fat in the bloody mess of what used to be his thigh. I had to look away for fear of embarrassing myself by vomiting over the manager's back as he sat in front of me in the dugout. Not that it would have been possible. Arthur was already on his feet and running towards his stricken player on the pitch.

All the while, throughout this horror, David lay still, accepting the situation. Until, that is, Arthur reached him and David started screaming in agony. The screams were so loud they silenced the murmuring crowd and shocked Arthur.

'Jesus Christ, son! Compose yourself, David! You'll be alright!'

David didn't hear him. He was still squealing. Arthur tried again in a calmer tone.

'Come on, son. Pull yourself together. Come on now.'

David stopped screaming and found his voice. He proceeded to utter six words that had the whole dugout in stitches with laughter. They're words I've never forgotten.

'Arthur, you're standing on my hair!'

On the topic of stitches, David required 60 to repair the damage done to his thigh that day. Arthur? He was more careful in future where he placed his feet while comforting long-haired footballers.

The Kevin Keegan effect: 1982-84

I never played with a footballer more professional than Kevin Keegan. Some respected commentators were postulating that the former England captain was coming to Second Division Newcastle United at the ripe old age of 31 to wind down his incredible career. How wrong they were! In his two-year spell, he was a phenomenon. Not just on the pitch either. He trained like a demon every day. He stayed behind in the afternoons to do extra work on his finishing, or other parts of his game he wanted to improve. He treated every player, every member of staff and every fan with great respect and good humour. He possessed an infectious enthusiasm and charisma that rubbed off on all those who met him and worked with him. He turned average players into good ones and transformed good ones, like Peter Beardsley and Chris Waddle, into great ones. He not only re-energised an ailing football club, he also galvanised the entire city of Newcastle. My boyhood idol didn't disappoint in the flesh. The great Bill Shankly once observed, 'Kevin Keegan is everything a man should be.'

Well said, Bill, well said!

A plastic pitch and a shopping trip

By January 1983 I'd become a regular part of the squad for the first team. I was 17. I'd started only one game, but I was always involved with the match-day squad. Most times I travelled in the knowledge that I'd be required for nothing more than to carry the skips from the bus to the changing rooms. On odd occasions, I'd travel knowing I was going to be the substitute. I'd either work it out based on my latest performance for the reserve team, or the manager, Arthur Cox, would tell me in advance.

For our upcoming fixture away to Queens Park Rangers on 15 January, I was certain I'd be travelling as a spare part. I hadn't played particularly well for the reserves that week. There were no fresh injury concerns with the first team. So when we made our way to the AstroTurf pitch behind Gateshead Stadium to play in a first team v reserve team practice match on the Thursday before the game, my biggest concern was not to injure myself on this strange new surface.

I didn't possess any 'special' AstroTurf boots, so I just wore my moulded stud boots. As we lined up I noticed that John Anderson, who was the first team right back marking me, was wearing his special AstroTurf boots. That freezing morning, I studied the feet of the other first team players and I didn't hold out much hope for my ragtag bunch of reserve team colleagues. The entire first team were wearing their special boots, while our team, with the exception of one or two, wore moulded studs. It was bad enough being inferior to players like Kevin Keegan, Terry McDermott and Chris Waddle, never mind having to compete against them in inadequate footwear. I suppose it made no sense for the club to fork out unnecessarily on AstroTurf boots for the entire playing squad, when only 12 pairs were required for those who played Queens Park Rangers, once a season, on the plastic pitch at Loftus Road. It still felt a little unfair that morning in Gateshead, though.

The game kicked off and, sure enough, Kevin Keegan, with his low centre of gravity and special boots, was dancing and skipping around our floundering defenders. His boots gripped onto the alien surface, while our tall centre-backs ice-danced and slipped and slid like Bambi over the frozen carpet. It felt like it was going to be a long cold morning for me hugging the left touchline, playing in a team that was unlikely to see much of the ball. Until, that is, I received my first pass of the day. The ball had barely reached my foot before John Anderson fell over as he tried to tackle me. I ran unopposed towards Jeff Clarke. I slowed as I approached him, and then quickly changed direction. He fell over too. I rounded the goalkeeper, Kevin Carr, and scored. The day just got better after that. It was like playing against statues. These usually tough-tackling, experienced defenders simply couldn't stand up, couldn't turn and couldn't make a tackle, even while wearing their special boots. My moulded studs gripped the surface well enough for me to twist and turn my way through one of the most memorable training sessions I ever had as a professional footballer. My low centre of gravity completely trumped their special boots. After the practice match I boarded the coach for the journey back to our Benwell base. Arthur was sitting alone on the front seat as I passed him.

'Jesus Christ, Paulie, son! You liked that bloody surface! The big boys couldn't handle you today. You'll be on the bench on Saturday, no question about that, son.'

My joy was spoiled by his firm slap across my freezing red thigh.

I was fizzing with anticipation when we stepped onto the AstroTurf at Loftus Road, on the Friday evening before our Saturday afternoon game. We didn't ordinarily train on the opposition's pitch the day before a game, but it made sense to do so on this occasion. Me, and my moulded studs, were full of confidence as we lined up for a five-a-side game with the other first team players and their special boots. The ball came to me. I controlled it and moved off all in one movement. Then I fell over. When I got off the hard floor I waited for another pass. I slipped over again as I tried to steady myself to receive it. Arthur shouted.

'Jesus Christ, son, stay on your feet. You're winning on points!'

That was just it: I couldn't stay on my feet. I couldn't stand up. When I did get to my feet, I'd fall over again as soon as I tried to change direction. The special boots worked on this surface. My moulded studs did not. The other glaring difference between Loftus Road and our practice pitch at Gateshead was how the ball bounced. On our training pitch, the ball bounced a little higher than it did on grass. On this pitch, it would bounce in front of me, I'd anticipate controlling it at chest height, but instead it'd fly high, right over my head. If it bounced in front of me as I tried to control it with my foot, it would skip up and hit me somewhere between my shin and my knee. Arthur stopped the session after my latest tumble.

'Go and change into your AstroTurf boots, son. You can't bloody stand up in yours.'

He was very annoyed when I told him I didn't possess any special boots.

'Well, you can't play in those, son. You'll have to buy a pair when the shops open.'

So on the morning of 15 January, 1983, when Newcastle United, Kevin Keegan et al. played QPR, I went shopping. I got on the Tube with Neil McDonald, my 17-year-old teammate. We walked up and down Regent Street, three hours before kick-off, trying to find a sports shop that sold AstroTurf boots. I bought a pair and wore them that afternoon in the Football League fixture.

I came on in the second half to replace Imre Varadi. I got the ball soon after coming on. My special boots gripped the surface. I knocked the ball around Bob Hazell and got ready to use my blistering pace to speed past him. He swatted me away like I was an annoying fly. We lost the game 2-0. The result had less to do with our boots than it did with the QPR ground staff laying tons of sand on the pitch since we'd trained on it the night before. The ball now bounced and moved off the surface entirely differently. Our players, all of them, were slipping and sliding all over the sanded surface. By the time we'd got accustomed to the change, John Gregory had danced around our statues, all in our special boots, to score his second goal. I never did wear those boots again.

Superman, the squadron leader, and a very angry Irishman

In the summer of 1983, Newcastle United embarked on a month-long trip to the Far East. We departed immediately after our final game of the season against newly promoted Wolves. An injury to Kevin Keegan had halted our own expected promotion push and we'd finished fifth, three points off the third promotion spot, which was claimed by Leicester City.

I have only two memories of that Wolves game. One was of Northern Irish footballing legend Derek Dougan (and Wolves chairman at the time) giving a rousing speech to the ecstatic fans before the game had even started. The team had already secured promotion and the game was a dead rubber. I was injured, having pulled my hamstring a few days before. The manager had decided to bring me along anyway, as I was included in the squad to travel to the Far East after the season finished. Instead of sitting bored in the changing room before kick-off, I stood in the sunshine of Molineux Stadium and soaked up the party atmosphere of the day. Dougan's speech certainly added to the occasion.

He was merely the hors d'oeuvre before the main course. I heard a loud roar to my left and turned just in time to see Superman, with his cape flowing behind him, sprinting towards the packed crowd behind the goal. When he'd reached the goalmouth, he began swinging wildly from the crossbar. He followed that performance with some other impressive acrobatics that had the crowd totally in his thrall. I thought it was part of a show, organised by Wolverhampton Wanderers, to celebrate the great achievement of gaining promotion to the First Division. I still thought that right up to the moment he donned his goalkeeping gloves and commenced diving around, palming away every ball the coach smashed in his direction. That was the first time I ever came across the extremely eccentric, but very likeable, John Burridge, who was the Wolves keeper that season. I would subsequently go on to work with him in the mid '90s, when I was a physio and he was a player and then a coach at Newcastle United. He was still performing his agility exercises even then – and was as fit, if not fitter, than the Premier League goalkeepers he trained with and later coached, including Pavel Srniček, Mike Hooper and a young Steve Harper.

He sold me some jeans out of the back of his car sometime in 1993. The dye that ran all over my legs when I wore them only fully came off sometime in 1994.

Despite the disappointment of missing out on what had been an expected promotion to the First Division, there was a buoyant atmosphere among the players and staff as we gathered outside St James' Park. It was the Monday after the Wolves game and we were about to embark on our month-long tour of the Far East. For a boy of 17 from my background, this was certain to be the trip of a lifetime. It also guaranteed I wouldn't be getting home to my family and girlfriend in Ireland as soon as I would have hoped – and when I did eventually get there, I'd be with them for a much shorter period of time than I'd have liked. Homesickness aside, I realised how lucky I was. Given that I had injured my hamstring the week before, Arthur Cox could just have easily left me at home and taken a fit player in my place. I think he had hopes that the injury was a minor strain and I'd be fit for the second half of the tour in Japan. It was obvious I would play no part in our first two games in Malaysia and the following two in Thailand. It may seem incredible that Newcastle United, a Second Division team, were invited in the first place. Until, that is, you factor in the presence of world superstar Kevin Keegan in our ranks. We were all getting a once in a lifetime experience solely because of Kevin.

We were waiting at St James' for the last few stragglers to arrive when a gold Lotus Esprit sped into the car park. The players murmured as the driver door opened and a sprightly septuagenarian sprung out. He threw his BOAC bag over his shoulder and bounced up the steps to where we were standing directly outside the main entrance to the stadium. Kevin Carr, our goalkeeper, whispered to the group.

'Fuck me, it's "Young" Mister Grace.'

If you're not familiar with *Are You Being Served?*, let me translate. Our latest travel companion was diminutive, balding, grey, but bursting with energy, enthusiasm and life. He cheerily greeted us as he bounded up the final step.

'Hello, chaps, what fettle?'

I had no idea what he was saying or who he was, and only learned about both from Kevin Carr as we boarded the coach on our way to Newcastle airport.

'He's one of our directors, James Rush. Squadron Leader James Rush to you and me, son.'

He explained the various meanings of *fettle* to me. Squadron Leader James Rush was in fine fettle that morning and he remained in fine fettle for the rest of the tour. He was especially fond of the hotel pool. From the moment we arrived in Malaysia to the moment we departed Japan a month later, I don't think I saw the squadron leader anywhere else but in the pool or at team dinners. He'd do length after length of breaststroke as we sat around marvelling at his stamina and fitness. My awe subsided a little only when Chris Waddle pointed out to the rest of the group that the squadron leader wasn't actually swimming but instead had one foot on the floor tiles of the pool at all times.

One foot on the ground or not, the aged squadron leader was a hugely impressive character, nonetheless. He made the most of his tour of the Far East. We all did, some more than others.

Pasty, white, Irish skin is not suited to being exposed to the baking heat of Thailand. I had already learned that painful fact when I'd burned my shoulder in the pool in Malaysia the week before. John Anderson, our right back, had not. John was an amiable Dubliner, with paler skin than me, if that's possible. He spent our rare day off lying by the pool having a few well-earned beers with his teammates. When they'd all departed the pool area, John fell asleep under the parasol. By the time he awoke, the sun had moved but the parasol hadn't. He was already in agony before he left the poolside. The following day and the day after that, his entire back was covered in the biggest, ugliest blisters I've ever seen. I've never witnessed sunburn like the sunburn

John Anderson had in Thailand in the summer of 1983. It was so severe, in fact, that the manager wanted to leave him out of the team for the match against the Thai national team. John, being a hardy Dubliner, would hear nothing of it and lined up in the baking heat of a Bangkok afternoon with the rest of the team. How he did that, I'll never know. The physio and the coach had to help him put his jersey on, careful not to touch the unburst blisters, or to scratch against the already burst blisters.

Ten minutes into the game, and a message came to the bench that our very brave full-back was in agony. John was wilting in the stifling heat. He didn't want to come off, but was asking for a bucket of cold water to be brought around to the far side of the pitch. He wanted to be doused with it to help cool the raging fire on his back. Arthur turned to me.

'Will your hamstring hold up to jogging around there with the bucket?'

Feeling useless and a little guilty for playing no part in the trip, I was already on my feet and on my way to give my stricken friend and teammate the relief he so desperately needed. The heat was so severe that I could hardly breathe as I jogged my way to John, trying desperately not to spill too much of his water before I got to him. I stood patiently at the side of the touchline with my bucket of icy water at the ready. There was a break in play. John lumbered wearily towards me. He half-turned, offering me his blistered back.

'Here, son. Throw it on. My back's on fucking fire.'

I readied my bucket, took aim at his back – and held on to the bucket for a fraction too long. I watched as the water sailed into the air and landed nowhere near its intended target. I'd always got on well with John Anderson, even when he would regularly kick lumps out of me in training. I like him still, and I'm sure he likes me. But I'm so glad that on that particular day in Thailand he wasn't able to leave the pitch to chase after me as I ran as fast as I could to get away from him. It's the only time in my life that I've been called a useless twat – and I agreed entirely. He threw some other words at me too, but I couldn't make them out. I was too busy running. I hurt my healing hamstring sprinting away from him and didn't play any part in the rest of the tour.

Sorry about the water, John!

The wisdom of Arthur

Arthur Cox is a remarkable man. He is also a very wise man. I'm sure any professional footballer who has ever had the pleasure of working with him during his long and distinguished career will share my sentiment. He was manager when I began my 18-year association with Newcastle United. He also returned as a trusted lieutenant of Kevin Keegan in the '90s. The Arthur I worked alongside in the '90s was a warm generous spirit who always had the interests of the players, staff and the club at heart. That same Arthur Cox is now in his ninth decade of life, yet he still calls me on a regular basis to check in with me: he asks how I am coping with my latest health concern, how my family is doing, how life is treating us in general.

Arthur is a kind man and a wise counsel. He was also a bloody scary man when I was a shy teenager in his charge. I'm sure he didn't mean to be so scary. I think the scariness was more to do with my state of mind. I was always keen to do well for him, I never wanted to disappoint him and I hung on every wise word he imparted. He imparted plenty of words on a daily basis. Some wiser than others.

It was preseason 1983. We were in Hamburg for a game, courtesy once again of Kevin Keegan. Hamburg had been his home for a spectacularly successful period in his career after leaving Liverpool. After playing no part in our end-of-season tour of the Far East, I was determined to hit the ground running when I came back from my short visit home. I had just turned 18 earlier in the month and was anxious to show Arthur that I'd heeded his words after he'd expressed his disappointment that I'd not taken part on the tour. I didn't have the heart to tell him that the reason I'd reinjured my hamstring was because I was sprinting away from John Anderson's wrath.

The game kicked off. I was in my usual place, sitting beside Arthur as a sub, and anticipating that I might get onto the pitch at half-time or maybe for the last 30 minutes. Two minutes had passed when Arthur pushed me off my seat.

'Get warmed up, you're going on.'

I ran up and down the touchline, stopping only to stretch my delicate hamstring. I looked around the pitch to see who was injured so early in the game. I couldn't see any obvious candidate. I glanced to the bench to see Arthur furiously calling me back to the halfway line. The physio put the numbers up. My friend, Neil McDonald, trudged dejectedly towards the touchline, trying to establish why he was being substituted after less than five minutes of the game. He hadn't quite turned 18, but was already a regular in the first team. We roomed together on away trips, two kids in a man's world. I shook Neil's confused hand and made my way across the pitch to left wing. One minute later, the ball went out of play for a corner kick. Then I saw another substitute on the touchline and waited for the physio to raise the numbers board. He did. I had to check it twice. It was Number 12 – me! I jogged towards Arthur trying to work out why I was coming off before I'd even touched the ball. I didn't have long to wait to find out. I walked down the tunnel. I reached the changing room just as Neil was coming out of the shower.

'Your hammy gone again?'

I shook my head as I answered.

'No. I've no idea why he took me off. I hadn't even touched the ball.'

The door opened behind me. Arthur looked at Neil, then he looked at me.

'You two boys. Too many bright lights and fancy hotels. That's your problem. Not hungry enough, the both of you. You think you've made it. That's the problem with the pair of you. If you lose the hunger, you won't survive in this game. D'you hear me?'

We both nodded. With that, the door closed behind him and he never spoke of it again. That wasn't the end of the wisdom of Arthur on that Hamburg trip, though.

I was with Neil in the dining room of our hotel. It was on the rooftop of a 20-storey building in the centre of Hamburg. We were the first to arrive for dinner, most probably because we were terrified of being late after our afternoon experience at the game. We were peering over the side of the balcony and watching the sunbathers below.

We didn't hear him come in. We didn't hear him walk over to where we were standing. We didn't even see him until his head appeared in between ours. Arthur looked down to see what we were staring at. He took a step back. Then he put one hand on my head and the other one on Neil's and banged our heads together, before imparting his second pearl of the day.

'Nothing down there for you boys. Sex? I've tried the lot. Jumping off wardrobes and all the rest of it. Most overrated pastime in the world. I'd sooner see a good cross and a great header any day of the week, I can tell you. Oh Christ, aye. Oh Christ, aye. Any day of the week. Don't you worry about that, boys.'

He left us there and laughed his way to the dining table. We rubbed our heads and smiled to each other. There was nothing else to do, or nothing else to say, after we'd just received our second dose of the day of the wisdom of Arthur.

Meeting an idol

I was glad to see the back of the 1983/84 promotion season. While it was an amazing one for Newcastle United it was a disaster for me. I spent most of the season injured or recovering from injury. My delicate hamstring seemed to tear every time I attempted to sprint at full pace. I'd know it was going to tear minutes before the dreaded moment it would inevitably do so. And I couldn't do anything to stop that from happening. When I was fit, I wasn't performing to anywhere near the standard of the previous two seasons. My confidence was low from all the injuries and my form when fit was nowhere near good enough to be anywhere close to the exciting promotion-chasing team, led by the combined brilliance of Keegan, Waddle and Beardsley.

I think the manager, Arthur Cox, ran out of patience. Peter Beardsley had arrived in the September, not long after the departure of fan favourite Imre Varadi. Peter was a revelation. I was mesmerised by his natural ability as a footballer and he was undoubtedly the best I ever played with. I still think to this day that his incredible talent is underrated. He could pass, he could tackle, he had a great footballing brain, but most of all he was in possession of mercurial dancing feet. He was mesmerising to watch and bamboozling to defend against. I've never seen a player quite like him. He was untouchable that promotion season, alongside Keegan, Waddle and McDermott. The only things I got from that season were some excess fat, a shocking new dress sense and a particularly crap 'beans on toast' haircut.

I was apprehensive as I returned from my summer break in preparation for the 1984/85 season. All had changed at the club. Kevin Keegan had retired, Arthur Cox had been replaced by Jack Charlton. I'd trained hard all through the summer in an attempt to shake off my hamstring troubles. I came back, nervous but ready to kick-start my stalled career. I trained well in Jack's early days. So much

MEETING AN IDOL

Mission accomplished. Kevin Keegan celebrates Newcastle United's promotion with teammates following a 4-0 win over Derby County in May 1984.

so, that I was quickly brought back into the first-team picture. More importantly, I felt like I was worthy of being there again.

I was full of excitement and anticipation when I was included in the squad to face Hibernian, on 5 August, for Jackie McNamara's testimonial. Not merely because it signified I was back in contention, but mainly because it meant I might get to step on to the same pitch as the legendary George Best. I was born in 1965, part of the generation who just missed out on seeing George at his genius best in the late '60s and early '70s, but who were totally captivated by his legendary status. Long before I even knew he was a footballer, I can still remember every word of the less than complimentary song we all sang while playing in the same Ulster streets from which he'd once emerged. It was sung to the melody of 'Superstar', from the rock opera *Jesus Christ Superstar*.

Georgie Best
Superstar
He wears frilly knickers and a see-through bra...

We didn't see George before the game, but we knew he was definitely playing when Jack gave his team talk. He turned to our defenders as he spoke.

'Don't worry too much about the drunk fella. He's 38 and he pissed his career away by the time he was 28. He's only here to sell tickets.'

I took my usual place on the bench, but was happy just to be back in contention. I was very excited to see my name on the same match day programme as Georgie Best Superstar. Jack's harsh words were still running around in my head as the game kicked off. When it did, I couldn't take my eyes off George. He jogged around, getting the occasional touch of the ball, to rapturous cheers from both sets of fans. He was clearly out of condition and it was obvious that Jack's blunt prematch assessment was entirely accurate. I'd have to satisfy myself with video footage of the greatest player in Irish history and one of the greatest of all time. His genius was consigned to the archives.

Then, 10 minutes into the game, he picked the ball up on the edge of our box. He moved his hips and the first defender moved with them. He approached the second defender. He moved his hips the other way and the defender followed them. He drew the goalkeeper to him and knocked the ball around him towards the goal. It hit the inside of the post and came back out again. It had all happened so fast, and so rhythmically, it was like I was watching ballet for a moment. We sat, open-mouthed, as Jack laughed and slapped the top of the dugout.

'Fuck me. Did you see that? The boy's a genius!'

George did nothing much after that. He didn't need to. It was a beautiful glimpse of what the world had seen, all those years before, while I was singing derogatory songs in the playground. George came into the player's lounge after the game. Compared to us mortals, he looked and dressed like a Hollywood superstar. He had his young son with him. He drank a Coke and made a speech, telling everyone in the room that his drinking days were behind him. He was staying sober for his son. He toasted our beers with his Coke. I was introduced to him. I stood dumbstruck and starstruck as he talked to me about home, about Northern Ireland and about Bob Bishop, the scout who'd discovered him. Bishop was the man who'd sent me on the same journey to Manchester United, with Norman Whiteside, when I was 11 years old. George's parting advice to me was short and sweet.

'Don't get caught up with the drinking and all that goes with it. Just play your football.'

It was predictable but good advice.

I met George Best only once more after that day. It was 10 years later, in the Wellington Park Hotel Belfast, on the morning he was due to play against Newcastle United, in Billy Bingham's testimonial, on 12 August, 1994. I was Newcastle United's physio that day. I approached his table to say hello as he sat in the reception area. He was so drunk he could barely speak. He offered to buy me a drink. I declined. He played in the game three hours later. As he entered the field of play, I'm not sure he knew where he was. I don't know how many touches of the ball he got, or how he played that day. It was too painful to watch. I couldn't watch that day, but I have watched him many times since thanks to footage that is old and dated now – and there is no denying his genius. In an era where defenders were practically permitted to commit assault, it is a thing of real beauty to watch George Best shrug them off, glide around them and then raise one hand aloft to celebrate as the ball rolls into the net once more. My childhood song started accurately enough:

Georgie Best
Superstar. . .

It should have just ended there, too.

The man in the white coat

Modern-day Newcastle United is no different to any other Premier League football club. There is a huge support staff on hand to ensure the playing staff are in the best possible condition. The backroom staff at the club consists of six physiotherapists, two doctors, three soft tissue specialists, five strength and conditioning coaches, twelve analysts, seven coaches and six kitmen. The Newcastle United I joined in the early '80s was a very different organisation. There was a manager, two coaches, a physiotherapist, a part-time chief scout and a part-time doctor. That was it. Well, not quite. That was it in terms of support staff *at the training ground*. There was also a man at St James' Park. He wore a long white coat and his name was Alec. He seemed to live in the treatment room just off the home changing room. I can never remember going into that area without him being there to greet me. It was his domain.

Alec Mutch was a permanent fixture during my five years as a player. For the first year I was there, he was ably assisted by an equally pleasant man, Benny Craig, a former player now employed alongside Alec as a trainer. And Alec was definitely a trainer, I knew that much. I just could never really work out what a trainer did. We had coaches and a physio at the training ground and a trainer at the stadium. Alec appeared to be part physio, part masseur and part kitman. Whatever he was, he was a wonderful man, full of good humour and kindness. I spent one brilliant afternoon chatting with him in his treatment room at the stadium. It transpired that he and his family had a remarkable history with Newcastle United. Alec had been employed as the trainer for over 40 years (over 50 by the time he passed away in 1987). Before that, his father Sandy was a goalkeeper in the 1920s, who became the groundsman for 34 years after he retired. When Sandy died, Jackie Milburn commented, 'The players thought the world of him.'

Before that afternoon speaking with Alec, I had only ever approached him when my boots were damaged. He'd study them hard before deciding that they should go to the cobbler rather than be replaced. Trying to convince him I needed a new pair from the sports shop in the city centre, owned by chairman Stan Seymour, was futile. On the very rare occasion he did relent and agreed that a new pair of boots were in order, I'd head off to the shop with a note from Alec informing the staff there exactly what boots I was allowed. It was strictly Adidas Europa Cup for reserve team players; Adidas World Cup was for the first team. It was a proud day when I got my first note for Adidas World Cup!

Much of my confusion around what role Alec performed stemmed from an early interaction with him. In only my second appearance for the youth team as a 16-year-old, I sustained a nasty cut on the top of my head, courtesy of backing into a full-back's tooth. I was patched up at the training ground, where the game took place. I'd thought I'd be heading off to the local hospital, but instead I was driven to the stadium to meet with Alec. Dressed in his white coat, he studied the wound. He mumbled something about it being 'a four or five job', then disappeared. He came back wheeling a trolly. It had some stitching equipment and a bottle of whisky on it. He pulled on some sterile medical gloves, poured a large glass of whisky and held it towards me as he pulled the trolley. The smell of the whisky made me nauseous. I shook my bloodied head at him,

'I'm 16. I don't drink whisky.'

He looked at me and laughed. Then he looked at the whisky.

'This? Don't worry, son. This is not for you. This is to steady my hand.'

With that, he took a large gulp and proceeded to insert four eye-watering stitches into my scalp. I still have a lump on my head to this day. Alec Mutch was a great man and a wonderful servant to Newcastle United. I'm still not sure about his stitching technique, though.

'Did we score that one?'

8 September, 1984. We played Manchester United at Old Trafford. We'd won three of our four games back in the top division; they'd drawn their first four games. We arrived full of hope. I was thrilled to be in the squad. The first club I'd ever had trials with was Manchester United. I was 11 years old when I'd spent a week there with Norman Whiteside, at the behest of Bob Bishop, the scout who'd sent the legendary George Best on the same journey. Old Trafford was also the first professional football stadium I'd ever set foot inside. I was there in March 1976, when Manchester United defeated the mighty Leeds United by three goals to two. I was a Liverpool fan as a boy, but that day, that moment, when I first glanced down at the Old Trafford pitch, has stayed with me all of my life. That was the moment when I promised myself that one day I'd come back to this famous old stadium and be one of the tiny figures running around on the brilliant green patch in the middle of the deafening crescendo. That exhilarating game passed by me in a blur. The noise stayed with me, though. The noise when a goal was scored was like nothing I'd ever heard before. The roar from the Stretford End each time the home team scored had resonated in my chest before it had subsequently blown the roof off. I may well have been a Liverpool fan, but I travelled home from that trip with photos of my new heroes – Gordon Hill, Sammy McIlroy and David McCreery.

Now I was back. And one of my heroes of that day, David McCreery, was my teammate. Norman Whiteside was now a permanent and brilliant fixture in the Manchester United team. Getting off the team coach that September day in 1984 was a proud moment. Even though I was 13th man and unlikely to play any part, I was back – back in the place where I'd promised my 11-year-old self I would be. I felt 10 feet tall as we made our way past the memorial plaque dedicated to the victims of the Munich air disaster. I couldn't wait to get into the changing room and then down the tunnel onto the piece of grass I'd only ever seen from on high as a starstruck boy in March 1976.

Our three wins in four games meant that the team made its way into the famous stadium full of confidence and hope. As the players got changed, I stepped back out into the narrow corridor outside the changing rooms. I'd noticed a payphone there and I called home. For no other reason than to tell my mum and dad that I was calling them from the corridor outside the changing rooms at Old Trafford!

As I was talking to my mother, my confidence took a bit of a knock. The home changing room door opened and Mark Hughes, the young Manchester United centre-forward, emerged. He was wearing his shorts and socks and nothing else. He began jogging up and down past me, quite the sight. He had the torso of a middleweight boxer and his shorts were rolled up, exposing the biggest thighs I'd ever seen on any footballer. He ran past me with an expression on his face that suggested he might kill anyone who was stupid enough to get in his way. He was less than two years older than me, but miles ahead of me in his physical and mental development as a footballer.

A steward tapped me on the shoulder while I was still on the phone telling my confused mother how well Mark Hughes was looking. He told me there was someone outside asking to speak to one of the Newcastle United party. I followed him to the door. There I shook hands with a 30-something man. The man asked if I could get him two tickets for the match. He was clearly a little embarrassed to be asking. He told me that he used to play for Newcastle United. He said I wouldn't remember him, but some of my older teammates might. I asked him his name. 'I'm Tony Green.' I told him that not only did I remember him, but everyone at Old Trafford inside the away changing room and in black and white in the stadium remembered him. Tony Green was, and still is, a Newcastle United legend. I got him his tickets. It was an honour to do so.

I was given another role that day. Our manager, Jack Charlton, asked me if I wouldn't mind looking after a blind Newcastle fan. I agreed. When the time came, I escorted the fan along the touchline to our ringside seats in the cauldron of noise. He was very charming and very excited to be sitting right next to the dugout. He asked me to explain how the teams were lining up, who was playing where and who was kicking towards the Stretford End. The game commenced. There was a crunching tackle and an increase in the noise rolling from the stands. He asked me to describe what had happened. So I did, and that was the pattern set for the entire afternoon: I was to be his eyes. It was all very well, and in fact was all going very well, until the goals started flying in. Into our net.

We lost 5-0 that day. Every time Manchester United scored, Old Trafford would erupt into ear-splitting noise, just like it had when I'd watched as a boy. A home goal at Old Trafford creates quite the buzz. Except, I suppose, if you are blind. Every time the stadium exploded, my blind friend would shout hopefully into my left ear, 'Did we score that one?'

By the time the fourth goal went in, it was pretty obvious, from the sheer volume of noise created, that the home team had scored again. But it was not so obvious to my shouting friend.

'Did we score that one?'

I told him the next time a goal was scored, he should perhaps listen for the level of the roar of the crowd. If it was a really loud roar, encompassing the entire stadium, then Manchester United had scored. If it was more muted and coming from a small section of the stadium, then we had scored. He was blind; he wasn't deaf! The fifth goal finished off the rout.

'That was them again, wasn't it?'

Mark Hughes, the middleweight boxer with the big thighs and the death stare, scored one of the goals obviously.

'You probably don't remember me...'

Jack Charlton managed Newcastle United for one season, 1984/85. I can vividly recall his first day at the club. He walked into our Benwell training ground, dressed head to toe in his hunting, shooting, fishing gear. He didn't bother changing out of that attire for the rest of the day. He stood at the side of the training pitch sipping his coffee. He spilled most of it, repeatedly stopping practice to bark his orders as to how he wanted his team to play. It didn't matter whether you were, like me, a youngster desperately trying to impress, or Peter Beardsley or Chris Waddle, two of the best players in the country. If you weren't carrying out Jack's game plan, you were getting both barrels while he spilled his coffee over his loafers.

His style of play didn't endear him to a lot of the senior players, or to the fans. His tenure, managing his boyhood club, was therefore a lot briefer than he had imagined when Jackie Milburn had helped persuade him to replace the recently departed Arthur Cox in June 1984. Fourteen months later Jack stormed out of the home dugout during a preseason friendly after he'd heard a small pocket of fans calling for him to go. 'Fuck that. I don't need this.' It's fair to say that few fans, or indeed players, were sorry to see the back of Jack Charlton and his direct style of play. I wasn't one of their number.

Jack Charlton was good for me and my development as a fledgling footballer. He liked my pace and the directness of my play on the left wing. I liked the simple instructions he provided about how he wanted his wingers to play. When I was fit enough (which wasn't often enough), I was included in most of his match-day squads. I scored my only senior goal under his management. I can still remember his very blunt and very clear instruction to me before I took the field at St James' Park that night in September 1984. Our opponents were Bradford City and their full-back was 36-year-old former Leeds United and England captain Trevor Cherry, an old teammate of Jack's.

'Ferrisy. Go on and have a run at Trevor. He'll not catch you, son. He's slower than me.'

I did exactly what Jack had told me to do. Not long after entering the field of play, I raced on to a ballooning high ball that had been flicked on by Chris Waddle. Trevor Cherry's brilliant but ageing legs couldn't keep up with my excited and youthful ones. I thumped the bouncing ball past the advancing Bradford City goalkeeper and experienced one of the most exhilarating moments of my entire life. I had scored a goal at the Gallowgate End of St James' Park! I thought it might be the first of many, but in the end it proved to be the highlight of an abruptly curtailed career. And if the goal was mine, it was also Jack's – a goal straight out of the Jack Charlton playbook.

The manager was very complimentary about me in the press afterwards. In private, he made it clear to me that I would be a big part of his plans moving forwards. Most of the remainder of my season was ruined by several injuries, but Jack was always a source of encouragement. He liked me as a player and told me so on numerous occasions. That's why I was one of the few who were disappointed to see him leave.

The day he left, in August 1985, wasn't the last time I crossed paths with Jack Charlton. When I returned to Newcastle United as a physiotherapist in 1993, he was a regular visitor to the training ground, and to the stadium, in his capacity as Ireland manager. He still lived in the north-east and was also often present at the many sporting awards dinners held in the region. I was in his presence on numerous occasions in all of those settings and I was always grateful to him as he had given me my best moment in football. Once, I was at an awards dinner at the Civic Centre, in Newcastle, where Jack was the star guest. I was physio for Newcastle and he was managing Ireland. Earlier in the evening, we'd been standing side by side, in the small VIP lounge, adjacent to the banqueting hall. As usual, Jack didn't acknowledge me. I very nearly introduced myself to him at one lull in the conversation, but hesitated for fear of embarrassing myself in front of the players and staff in the vicinity. The moment was gone.

Later that night, I found myself in the toilets with Jack as my only companion at the trough. He smiled. I looked right and left. There was no one else around. My opportunity had arrived. I finally, nervously, plucked up the courage to reintroduce myself to my old manager.

'My name is Paul Ferris. I used to play for Newcastle. I scored my only goal for you as a player a few years back. You probably don't remember me.'

Jack Charlton studied my face. Then he shook his head and laughed.

'Aye, you're right, lad, I don't remember you!'

With that he was gone. I looked right and left again. I was glad no one else was there to witness our exchange. I saw Jack Charlton many more times after that. He smiled and nodded every time. I did likewise. I never tried to introduce myself to him again. I still have my goal at the Gallowgate End, though. Thanks for that, Jack.

The Gallowgate roar

St James' Park, perhaps more than any other stadium in the country, is famous for its passion, noise and singing. The mandatory transition to all-seater stadiums certainly had an impact on the atmosphere, not just at St James' but all around the country. Yet despite that, when St James' Park is really rocking, the feeling lingers in your bones.

Fans of a certain vintage talk of the atmosphere created in the Leazes End before it was demolished in the '70s. A giant roof-covered terrace, capable of housing 15,000 delirious Geordies, I can only imagine the noise it generated. In the '80s, it was all about the Gallowgate End – a mirror image of the Leazes, minus the roof, but what a roar it created in full voice! My first and abiding memory of that wall of sound was the day Kevin Keegan made his debut against Queens Park Rangers in August 1982. I'd arrived the season before when crowds averaged 17,000. I made my home debut in May 1982 when the attendance was even lower, just 10,000 disillusioned souls. The Gallowgate was half empty that day, with little clumps of diehards in 'the corner' and under 'the scoreboard' forced to sing to each other as they watched us limp to a 4-0 defeat. So before Kevin arrived, I had nothing to prepare me for what I would to witness on the afternoon of his debut.

Thirty-five thousand screaming Geordies greeted the teams onto the pitch. The singing and noise from the Gallowgate throughout the game was already like nothing I'd ever experienced before. Then Kevin exchanged headers with Imre Varadi and raced towards the Gallowgate, before slipping the ball around the advancing keeper and into the net. The Gallowgate erupted as one. The noise was deafening, the atmosphere intoxicating, the occasion unforgettable. I'd been a player at the club for 10 months and I already knew I was at a special football club, but witnessing that explosion of unbridled joy is what made me fall in love with Newcastle United.

I managed to score only one goal in my playing career at Newcastle United. One solitary goal. I scored it on a cold September evening in 1984. It was a goal that put us 2-1 up against Bradford City in a League Cup tie. It was at the Gallowgate End at St James' Park. If you are going to score only one goal in your professional career, what a place to do it! I can still remember the fleeting silence as the ball left my foot, then the deafening roar from the Gallowgate End which hit me like a punch in the middle of my chest. Like nothing I'd ever experienced before – or have experienced since. It was as if I'd been plugged into the National Grid. I couldn't breathe, I couldn't speak, I couldn't run. It was ethereal. If the Gallowgate roar can do that, what must the Leazes have sounded like with that same roar reverberating off the corrugated iron roof? I can only imagine.

Jack Charlton, a death threat and a missing gun

Jack Charlton was as famous for his hunting, shooting, fishing lifestyle as he was for his footballing achievements. I was sitting at the back of the team coach with Neil McDonald, on our way home from a preseason friendly in early August 1984. Jack came ambling towards us. He didn't sit down but towered above us as he spoke.

'How would you boys fancy making a few quid next Saturday?'

My first thought was that we must have a game that day. Jack assured us we didn't.

'I'll pay you twenty quid each for a couple of hours' work. Easiest money you'll ever make.'

Our blank faces ensured the Newcastle United manager was forced to elaborate.

'It's the Glorious Twelfth this weekend.'

Neil stared into space. I was more than a little confused. The only Glorious Twelfth I was aware of was commemorated in Northern Ireland, on the twelfth of July each year, to celebrate the Battle of the Boyne in 1690 – when William of Orange, the new Protestant king, defeated the forces of James II, the Catholic king who had only recently been deposed. As a Catholic boy, brought up in the predominantly Protestant town of Lisburn at the height of the Troubles, I'd never been overly keen on that particular piece of triumphalism. It was an occasion to keep your head down and stay indoors, particularly the night before, when rabid sectarianism, fuelled by cheap alcohol and bonfires, was a recipe for a good kicking if you were of the wrong persuasion.

I told Jack he was a month late for the Glorious Twelfth.

'No, you silly bugger. The Glorious Twelfth is the start of the grouse-shooting season. I'll give you twenty quid each to come grouse-beating with me next week.'

I had no idea what grouse-beating entailed, but it didn't sound like something professional footballers should be doing on their day off. Jack explained what it was and I was certain it wasn't something professional footballers should be doing on their day off.

'You just come along to the shoot. You'll get a big stick and go and flush the grouse out with it. You push them over the guns and we shoot them.'

Honestly, going to the traditional bonfire on the Eleventh Night sounded like a safer option for a Catholic boy in Northern Ireland. I didn't want to be anywhere near Jack, his mates and their shooting guns. I politely declined.

Evidence of Jack Charlton's love of hunting, shooting and fishing was everywhere. It was there in how he dressed every day, in the fishing waders and boots that cluttered his office, and in the occasional gun, or dead bird, that lay in the boot of his car. He loved the lifestyle and in many ways he was its poster boy. His fame and his very public support of that lifestyle drew the attention of various animal and bird protection activists, but his extracurricular activities were something separate from football. That is, until one afternoon in February 1985, when we were due to face West Ham at Upton Park.

The game was almost postponed, as protesters had scattered broken glass on the pitch in a protest against Jack's championing of blood sports. The vandalism of the playing surface was only part of the drama, though, on what was one of the strangest days I ever experienced as a footballer. On the morning of the game, the Met Police visited our hotel. Two senior detectives interrupted our team meeting to inform us that they had received a credible threat to Jack Charlton's life, which they were taking very seriously. There were lots of discussions about protecting Jack's safety, while we travelled to and from the game, should it go ahead. There would also be protection officers situated in and around our dugout. At one point it looked like the match was going to be postponed, before we got final word that the game was to take place as scheduled. We eventually travelled to Upton Park on a very surreal coach ride through London with Jack lying on the floor. All of the talk in our changing room was around the safety of Jack Charlton and, indeed, all of us. *What if someone smuggles a gun into the stadium and takes a potshot at our manager? What if they miss and hit one of us on instead?*

The final fragments of glass were removed from the playing surface as we were preparing for the game in the away changing room. The match finally kicked off. The game was in its early stages as West Ham attacked down our left flank. I was in the away dugout, seated behind Jack Charlton. Suddenly he stepped out of the dugout and began frantically gesturing towards the blue sky above Upton Park. I took my eyes off the game. I, too, searched the sky. I looked up just in time to see a flock of geese flying in perfect V formation over the head of our hunting, shooting, fishing manager. Jack turned to the dugout with his back to the action on the pitch. He stretched his arms up towards the sky in genuine exasperation.

'Ah bollox, would you look at that? Where's my fucking gun when I need it!'

I'm still not quite sure whether or not he was joking!

What were the chances of a flock of geese flying over Upton Park, that day of all days? I'm glad there wasn't a gun in Jack Charlton's vicinity. Can you imagine?

George Reilly wins a fight

George Reilly was a giant of a man. He was signed by Jack Charlton in early 1985 to be the focal point of the team's new style of play. He looked quite terrifying when he removed his front teeth, but the big Scot was a quietly spoken gentleman. He quickly became a popular member of the squad. He was someone I enjoyed being around, and great company on a night out as well. His mood never changed, whether he was smiling his way around our Benwell training ground, having lumps kicked out of him on a match day, or enjoying a pint or two with his teammates on a Saturday night in one of the many bars and nightclubs in Newcastle city centre.

On one particular night out after a game, the whole squad were in a nightclub. We'd drawn at home and a small group of disgruntled fans took umbrage at our presence. They felt our performance didn't merit us having a night out of any kind. It began as a bit of light-hearted ribbing. Then a big drunk, who was standing at the edge of the group, changed the tone. The more beer he consumed, the nastier his comments became. His mates were aware and tried to keep him in check, but he was too far gone. Every time any of our group walked past him, he'd have a comment to make.

'You're fucking useless.'

'You shouldn't be in here.'

'You should be ashamed to show your face after the way you played today.'

His friends tried their best, the bouncers tried their best and several Newcastle United players tried their best. It was all in vain. He wanted to fight, he was determined to fight and he knew who he wanted to fight. He honed in on his target, the smallest person in our group. As I tried to squeeze past him on my way to the bathroom, he grabbed hold of my forearm.

'Watch out, man. Say excuse me, you posing little twat.'

I tried to release my arm from his vice. He squeezed tighter.

'Can't even get in the team, but you can find your way out here all right. Think your God's gift. Nothing a good slap wouldn't fix.'

He was a terrifying bloke. His head was shaved, he was six foot tall and he had more muscles in his arm than I had in my entire torso. I was afraid of him. I didn't answer him. I tried once more to free my arm. He grabbed it tighter.

'What's the matter? Think you are too good to talk to the likes of me, you little prick? I pay your fucking wages. Don't you forget that.'

His mate helped break his grip on my arm. I was shaken by the experience and resolved that as soon as I left the bathroom, my night was over. I wasn't going back past him again. George Reilly was in the toilets when I got there. He read the fear in my face. He asked me what was wrong. I told him about the drunken idiot who'd just ended my night. George was adamant I wasn't going home. He told me to follow him out of the bathroom and said he'd lead me back to the safety of our group. I wasn't sure I wanted to, but I did what George asked. He passed the drunk, who completely ignored him. I tried to pass. The meathead stepped across me and blocked my path.

'Learned any manners yet, twat?'

I instantly regretted listening to George. I should've just gone home. I was mumbling some frightened nonsense back at my aggressor, but he was no longer listening. His attention was fully focused on George Reilly, who'd spun him around and was now holding him firmly by his fat throat. George, the quiet giant, had snapped.

'You and me, big man. Outside now!'

In full view of the bouncers, and half of the nightclub, Newcastle United's centre-forward frogmarched the man out of the club. They faced each other on the paved square just outside the front door. A huge crowd formed a ring around them. The two giants paced around each other like lions in a cage. Finally, George Reilly removed his false teeth. He walked over to his opponent. George pointed at his own chin as he spoke.

'Go on then, big fella. Give it your best shot.'

His opponent didn't hesitate. He wound his thick arm back behind him, before swinging it forward – and landed the most sickening punch I've ever seen, or heard, right on the point of George Reilly's chin. From the watching crowd came a collective gasp. I almost looked away, unwilling to see the gentle giant crumpled in a sorry mess on the pavement. I'm glad I didn't, though. To my – and everyone else's – astonishment, George Reilly never moved. He didn't rock back on his heels, he didn't fall to the floor. Instead, he absorbed the fierce blow, and simply stood there, staring at his assailant. George smiled a manic smile and stepped towards his stunned opponent.

'Is that the best you've got, big man?'

His aggressor took two steps back. Raised his hands in submission.

'You win, mate. I'm done.'

He disappeared through the crowd.

George Reilly took his false teeth from his pocket and placed them back into his recently punched mouth. We headed back into the nightclub. I couldn't really concentrate on my drink. I was too busy marvelling at George Reilly's granite chin. I'd just witnessed the only fight I've ever seen, before or since, where the winner was the person who hadn't actually thrown a punch.

Once Upon a Time in America

One huge upside of being part of the first team squad during the 1984/85 season was that I suddenly had a lot of money in my pocket. A new pay rise, regular appearance money and win bonuses ensured I had more than enough to waste on dreadful clothes and a ridiculous new haircut every other week. I'd been brought up in a typical working-class family. My father had always been in employment, and my parents made sure I wanted for nothing. We lived in a council estate in Lisburn, and we holidayed every summer in Donegal. Some of the accommodation we slept in wasn't exactly the Ritz. Looking back, I see clearly that money was tight. I'm very proud of the efforts and sacrifices they made looking after their family of seven children in circumstances that were undoubtedly tough. In truth, there was an abundance of love and laughter in my childhood home – and that love and laughter meant we were very rich in so many ways. I still miss those days.

Back in 1985, when I found myself with surplus money in my pocket, I wanted to share it with the people who'd given me everything in life. I made a few suspect purchases in my attempts to do so, though. My most dubious effort was the top-of-the-range teasmade I bought my slightly bemused parents. I think they used it twice before it sat gathering dust at my mother's side of the bed. VHS recorders were all the rage at the time, too. They were still a little too expensive for me to splash out on a purchase of one, so I rented one for my mother and father, for the period I was staying with them over the summer.

A lot had changed since I'd left home as a shy schoolboy. I'd developed from a boy to a young man. Those formative years are usually supervised by a boy's parents, who are there to nurture and to guide the child as he navigates the path to becoming a man. When I left home in 1981, my parents missed out on seeing their youngest boy grow, and I missed out on their love and support. I was forced to go it alone in a country that felt very alien. I was always desperate to spend time with my parents when the opportunity arose. I wanted to spend time with them for two reasons: because I missed them so much when I was away from them, but just as importantly I wanted them to see that the flashy dressing, mullet-topped young man who was back in their home was still the same person he'd been when he was living there with them. I wanted them to know that living in England for four years and playing professional football for Newcastle United hadn't changed me in any way. I wanted to show them that I hadn't lost sight of the values they'd taught me, and the love they'd showered on me. Renting the VHS recorder was an experience I could share with them.

We were all excited to watch our first video together. We just had no idea what to watch. Two middle-aged, conservative, Catholic parents, and a 20-year-old professional footballer who hadn't been to mass since the day he'd set foot in England, don't necessarily share the same taste in films. I walked the short distance from our home to the video rental store. It was opposite St Patrick's Church, on Chapel Hill. I spent half an hour reading the back of every box in the small shop, trying to find something that would appeal to us all. I gave up and thanked the confused man behind the counter for nothing. I opened the door and bumped straight into my older brother Joseph. He was on his way into the pool hall next door. Fifteen years older than me, he had spent much more time with my parents than I had. Surely he would know what they liked to watch?

He replied immediately and with a confident certainty.

'*Once Upon a Time in America*. Robert De Niro is in it. He's my Da's favourite actor. Me and Audrey watched it the other day. It's brilliant.'

I was grateful for his recommendation, but just had to double-check it was suitable for me to watch it with them.

'No problem, son. That's your film. They'll love it.'

Later that evening, my mother, my father and I settled down to watch our first ever video together. Two strict Irish Catholic parents and a mullet-topped professional footballer. Five minutes into the film, I started to feel a little uncomfortable with the swearing. Thirty minutes in, I was starting to sweat, and my mother was starting to shake her head. My father began tut-tut-tutting about an hour into it – and never stopped. His head was shaking in unison with my horrified mother's, while me and my mullet squirmed through the entire three hours, forty minutes of swearing, brutal violence and rape scenes. I could feel my mother's eyes boring into me during the second graphic rape scene. I barely even saw that scene. I still had my eyes half closed, pretending to be asleep, after the first rape scene! When my torture was over and the credits put me out of my misery, my parents didn't say a word. They got up, kissed me goodnight, and left me staring, shell-shocked, at the blank TV screen.

I put *Once Upon a Time in America* back in its box. I was certain I could hear my brother Joseph laughing all the way from his house. It was a great film, alright. It just should have come with a warning sticker:

DO NOT WATCH IN THE PRESENCE OF YOUR IRISH CATHOLIC PARENTS. ESPECIALLY IF YOU ARE TRYING TO DEMONSTRATE THAT YOU HAVEN'T BEEN CORRUPTED IN ANY WAY SINCE YOUR MOVE TO ENGLAND.

My head-shaking mother and tut-tut-tutting father doubtless climbed into bed that night wondering just how much their youngest son had changed since he'd moved to England . . . They didn't have to wait long to find out.

'Is Geraldine there?'

I met Geraldine McCaugherty when she was 13 years old. I was 14. It would prove to be by far the most significant meeting of my life. Geraldine was my girlfriend for seven years and has been my wife for thirty-eight years. It has been the greatest joy of my life to share my journey with her.

Since my move to England when I was 16, we had rarely spent any time together. We saw each other only when I could get a break from my football career. That was usually only in the off season and occasionally for a few days at Christmas, though that was less often the more involved I was with the first team. We kept our young love alive through nightly phone calls and weekly letters. We have a suitcase in the attic filled with our juvenile outpourings of love and angst. I haven't got the nerve to go back and read them. I'm sure when I eventually do they will provide as much embarrassment as they will entertainment. Especially the many I chose to write on black paper with my silver pen. The dab of Denim aftershave splashed over the page before closing the envelope will hopefully have worn off after 40-odd years. We were kids when we parted. Our early dates involved long walks, stopping to buy crisps and Curly Wurlys to share on the bench by the lake at Hillsborough Forest. She sucked her crisps, because she was too embarrassed to crunch them. I never shared my Curly Wurlys with her. I still don't!

In the summer of 1985, I had just turned 20 and Geraldine was 18. In the previous four years we had grown from kids to young adults. We hadn't seen each other for 10 months. Crisps and Curly Wurlys had lost a little of their lustre. We had other things on our minds. OK, I did still think about Curly Wurlys quite a lot, too. The previous four years had changed us both mentally and physically beyond all recognition from the kids we were when we had our first date at St Patrick's youth club. That night I'd bought a packet of Doublemint in case I got lucky. . . I didn't.

In the heat of July 1985, we agreed we wanted to take our clothes off. We just had nowhere private to do so. We were desperate to be alone, but trying to find time to be alone when both sets of parents were Irish Catholics was like trying to outwit the secret police. We loved each other with a passion. Passion and unmarried Catholic kids were to be kept well apart in 1985. An Irish Catholic mother could sniff that sort of nonsense out – and would do everything in her power to snuff it out. That summer, we still couldn't manage to spend time alone together in the sitting room of my home without my mother knocking on the door every 10 minutes. She'd open the door with her backside, then she'd flick on the light, even though the room wasn't all that dark to begin with.

'I've made you some tea and sandwiches.'

Always tea and sandwiches and always within 10 minutes of us entering the sitting room. She must have made the bastards in advance. We'd no sooner eaten the sandwiches and turned our attention to more important things than she'd be back again, as if by magic, holding two plates full of potato apple bread. She was riddled with angina, but Jesus Christ could she shift when she wanted to get into that sitting room! How fast can someone make potato apple bread, for fuck's sake?

At least we actually had the sitting room in my house with all of its interruptions. Geraldine's house was a no-go area entirely. Her mum was Mary – very obviously named after the Virgin Mary. If it weren't for the presence of her dad Leo, seated in his favourite chair in the living room, the house could easily have been mistaken for a nunnery. There were more holy relics in that house than there were in St Patrick's church up the road. Everywhere you sat, Jesus Christ had a good view of you. If he wasn't watching you, then Mary was . . . both of them. That summer was the most frustrating of our lives. It was desperate. So we took desperate measures. We needed to outwit Jesus, the Virgin Mary and the parents. We came up with a plan. It was a bloody good one, too. It had to be!

I told my mother I was going to stay at my friend's house. She didn't even question me. I hadn't seen my best friend all year, so why wouldn't I go and stay with him for a night? Geraldine had a more risky challenge. She had to tell her parents she was going to stay at my house and hope her mother or father didn't call my mother to confirm. We spent a nervous afternoon at my house waiting for the call from Mary that would have the secret police all over us. The phone rang several times that afternoon. Each time, my heart leapt into my throat and remained there until it was clear we hadn't been rumbled. The night finally came and we both stayed at my friend's house. Being there with Geraldine, with the real world locked outside our tiny room, was one of the happiest nights of my entire life. I never wanted it to end. But like all good things . . .

We decided it would be best if Geraldine left very early, and made her way home, before her parents had time to get out of bed and think about checking in on their daughter's welfare. We estimated that if she left at 7 a.m., then we'd be safe and everyone else would be none the wiser. Geraldine had only just closed the front door of my friend's house behind her, when his phone rang. It was my mother. My heart skipped. Her tone did little to correct my heart's rhythm.

'Is Geraldine there?'

My heart skipped again, but I told her the technical truth.

'No.'

She persisted.

'Has she been there?'

My heart stopped skipping and sank instead. I told her the truth again. What else can you do when they're on to you? I'd never lied to my mother. She had told me many years before that she could tolerate most things in life, but never lying. She summoned me home. That short walk from my friend's front door to my back door was torture at its worst. I felt physically sick as I opened the door to be confronted by my diminutive but fierce mother waiting for me at the kitchen table. I loved her dearly and never wanted to disappoint her in any way. The look on her face that morning left me in no doubt that I'd done just that with my scheming. She sent me off to bed with a shake of her head.

'I'm sure you'll need the rest after the night you've had!'

I was glad to escape to my childhood bedroom. I was still walking on shaky legs when she called me down the stairs five hours later. Geraldine was sitting in our living room when I got there. I half expected her mother to be on the settee behind the door – and was more than relieved when she wasn't. My mother followed me into the room and spoke to Geraldine.

'You put me in a terrible position this morning. I lied to your mother for you. Don't ever put me in that position again.'

That was it. That was all she said. What she didn't say was that she had been woken unexpectedly from her sleep by a phone call from Geraldine's mother. She had quickly unscrambled her brain and lied on Geraldine's behalf to save her the wrath of her mother.

Mary had asked if Geraldine was awake. My mother, who'd had previous experience of six children before me, simply replied that Geraldine was still asleep. Then having a fair idea of where Geraldine had spent the night, she phoned me to enquire as to her actual whereabouts. Without her quick thinking, and willingness to cover for us, it could have been a hell of a lot worse for us both.

I think I went down in her estimations that day. She, on the other hand, soared in mine.

I will always be grateful to my devout Catholic mother for lying on our behalf to Geraldine's devout Catholic mother. The alternative would have been unthinkable.

The character and kindness of 'Zico'

Professional football, especially in the '80s, was an unforgiving, harsh, sometimes brutal environment. A misplaced pass in training could lead to a volley of abuse from a senior player, a mistake in a game could result in a barrage of vitriol from the nearby paddock. Mick Martin was the club captain when I joined. A seasoned professional and an Irish international, he was someone for me to look up to as a boy who'd recently washed up at the club from across the Irish Sea. Although an obviously talented footballer with an incredible pedigree (his dad Con was a legendary international footballer), Mick was the go-to target for the boo boys at St James' Park in my first season. Every misplaced pass, or mistimed tackle, was pounced upon. It was uncomfortable to watch at times. Yet, despite the difficulties he was having, I don't recall a day at training where he didn't take time to ask me how I was doing or how my parents were keeping back home. He'd often stretch and warm up in my vicinity so that he could offer words of wisdom and encouragement. They were precious words for me to cling to, and I was grateful he took the time.

If his comforting words off the pitch showed great kindness, what he did on the pitch revealed a man of immense character. Rather than shy away from the bile of the boo boys, he continued to play his game the way he always had. The arrival of better players in Kevin Keegan and Terry McDermott elevated his game to a whole new level – so much so that the home fans christened him 'Zico' after the legendary Brazilian superstar, one of the greatest players in the world at that time. Mick became an integral part of the promotion-winning side of Keegan, Waddle and Beardsley in 1984. As a lonely homesick boy, I greatly valued his kindness. As an aspiring professional footballer, I was in awe of his character.

Joe Harvey's knees

Joe Harvey was once a sergeant-major in the Royal Army Physical Training Corps. He is also one of the most successful figures in Newcastle United's history: an FA Cup-winning captain, in 1951 and 1952, and until Eddie Howe the last manager to ever win a trophy for the club (Fairs Cup, 1969). I met him in 1981, on the first day I arrived at the club. I had no idea who he was, or what he'd achieved for the club. That day, to a young homesick boy from Ireland, he was just a friendly old man, who shook my hand as I sat dazed and confused in the communal area of our Benwell training ground. He wasn't even that old, but when you're 16, 60 is ancient. He was the club's chief scout, and a close confidant of manager Arthur Cox. Arthur had the air of a sergeant-major, and Joe had been a sergeant-major. On reflection, they were amazing individuals to guide any young player. Honour, integrity, respect and discipline were high on the agenda at Newcastle United in the early '80s. That first day, Joe Harvey, this great man who'd won trophies as a player and as a manager, sat down beside me. He patted my homesick knee. And spoke with a raspy Yorkshire twang.

'You're a long way from home, son. But you've come to the right club. Special place is this. Arthur will look after you. Keep your head down, work hard, you'll be reet. I'll keep an eye on you.'

I was too befuddled by my sudden move from home to a foreign land to appreciate the kindness of the gesture from this great man who'd achieved so much for the club as a player and manager.

Joe Harvey was true to his word. He did keep an eye on me. He did more than that, though. He was never one for faint praise, but he would often pull me aside after a game and have a word with me about what I'd done well and where I could improve. I quickly progressed to the reserve team. Joe would come to the away games. On the long coach journeys home, he'd sometimes make his way to me. He'd sit and talk through the game and my performance. If I'd played well, or scored a particularly good goal, he'd let me know he approved without ever going overboard.

'Was that really you? I had to check my eyes. Did you control the ball first time in the crowded penalty area, then have the composure to bend into the far corner? Bloody hell. Didn't think you had that in your locker. Good effort, that. More of that, son. I'll have to tell Arthur about that.'

He did tell Arthur. I'm sure he must have told him many times. I made my debut for the first team on 1 May, 1982. I was 16 years and 294 days old – the youngest player ever to play for the club. Joe Harvey's reports from those reserve games played a big part in that. I spoke with Arthur Cox recently about the events around that time and my debut match against Blackburn Rovers.

'Joe just said, "Arthur, if he is good enough, he's old enough, and the boy's good enough."'

It wasn't plain sailing for me after my debut. I picked up a series of niggling injuries, lost my confidence, and my form dipped for a while. Then I found myself out of the first team picture altogether. During that demoralising period, Joe Harvey never gave up on me. He still sat with me, on occasion, on the journey back from reserve games. He still critiqued my performance as we ate our fish and chips. I never felt like a lost cause when I spoke with him. Quite the opposite. I felt like a professional footballer. I felt empowered. When I forced my way back into contention at the beginning of the 1984/85 season, Joe was the first to pat me on the back. The night I scored my only senior goal, he sat down beside me in the changing room. He patted my leg.

'Was that you? I had to check my eyes. Did you race onto that pass and thump one past the keeper? Did you hear the noise from the Gallowgate? Special club this, son. Keep your head down. Work hard. You'll be reet.'

Those brief conversations with Joe Harvey didn't mean all that much to me as a 16-year-old, who'd just landed in an alien world, or as a 19-year-old, who'd just scored what he thought was destined to be the first of many goals at the Gallowgate End of St James' Park, but they mean so much to me now that I'm approaching the age he was when

I met him. They were brilliant words from an amazing man who, I recognise now, was simply an incredible man manager.

Joe Harvey was there the day I shattered my left knee in training, just days before the beginning of the 1985/86 season. It was a horrible injury, one that would eventually end my playing career. I knew it was bad from the moment I felt the searing pain, and heard the loud pop in my knee, as my rotating body weight broke through the defences of my knee ligaments. The pain was so severe, it made me vomit. I was still in considerable distress when I was carried into the treatment room. I was glad to see Joe when he came into the treatment room while my mangled knee was being assessed. In his usual brusque but kind manner, he made a valiant attempt to cheer me up. He rubbed his hand up and down my swollen knee. He had the weary air of a man who'd seen it all before and was therefore wondering what all the fuss was about. The tears that escaped from my eyes told me there was an awful lot to fuss about. Joe saw them and moved his hand from my knee to my wet cheek. He spoke to me and the physio in his gruff Yorkshire accent.

'Ah . . . it's just a bloody scratch, man. Kids today. Soft as bloody shite. In my day I'd have played on with that. We'd have stuck a bit of ice on there, got the doc to jab it, and all would be reet.'

He held his hand on my cheek. His resting hand said more about him, and the predicament I was in, than his words. I appreciated his efforts to ease my obvious fears for my future. His words were an attempt to offer comfort and I took solace from them. Maybe it was just a scratch? Maybe Joe Harvey was right and the kids of my day were just soft as shite? Maybe I could just stick some ice on it, have a jab, and play on like Joe had? After all, it hadn't done him any harm, had it? I'd almost started to convince myself. Then Joe Harvey let go of my cheek. I watched him wince in pain, before he hobbled slowly out of the room on his two bandy legs and completely ruined knees.

Maybe playing on with some ice and a jab from the doctor, wasn't the best advice the great man ever gave me. As for the rest of Joe Harvey's wise words, I appreciate them more now than I ever did back then. I regard it as an honour that he took the time to share them with me.

Jack Charlton's way. George Reilly dominates the St James' Park airspace in 1985. The contrast in style of play from the promotion season the year before proved impossible for many fans to accept.

'Is that Spandau Ballet?'

The summer of 1985 was the most significant summer of my life. After a year of pleading with her mother and father, and four years of living apart, Geraldine's parents reluctantly agreed that she could move to England to be with me. She was 18 years old. I am forever grateful to Mary and Leo McCaugherty for that decision. It shaped the rest of my life. I didn't fully appreciate at the time just how difficult and heart-wrenching that must have been for them. I was more focused on my own needs. I was desperate for her to come to me. I loved her, I missed her, and I was soul-crushingly lonely. I had made many friends in Newcastle. I was very familiar with the city after four years living there and the Geordies were a welcoming bunch. But none of that matters when the person you love most in the world, and indeed all of your family, is living across the Irish Sea.

Looking back now I can see how young we must have appeared to our parents. We were young, no doubt about that, but we knew what we wanted. We wanted to be together. The timing seemed perfect: my fledgling career looked to be heading firmly in the right direction. I was now an established part of the first team group. If the recently departed Jack Charlton had been good for my development, then I had every reason to believe that the recently appointed caretaker manager, Willie McFaul, would be even better. He'd always been a staunch supporter of me since the day I'd landed in Newcastle. A fellow Ulsterman, he had often pushed hard for me to be more involved with the first team.

All was pointing in the right direction in the weeks leading up to Geraldine's arrival. All, apart from my left knee. Now, just two days before Geraldine joined me for our new life together, I'd twisted it badly – and it was definitely pointing in the wrong direction. I didn't know it at the time, but my career was effectively over before Geraldine even set foot in Newcastle. I would never play in the first team again, and within 14 months I was out of professional football for good. I still regret that Geraldine never got to see me play at St James' Park. I would have loved to have shared that life experience with her.

Still, she was once in the capacity crowd when I scored my best ever goal, while playing for Northern Ireland against Wales in a youth international fixture in Belfast. After the game we travelled home to Lisburn in the back of her dad's car. I was so proud to have scored such a spectacular goal in front of my girlfriend. As we made our way out of Belfast, I waited for the moment when my equally proud girlfriend would congratulate me. I'd then shyly thank her and tell her it was nothing special at all. We were nearly in Lisburn and she still hadn't mentioned the goal. We'd talked about everything else but the goal. All I wanted to talk about was the bloody goal. It was the best goal I'd ever scored. I couldn't hold it in any longer.

'You haven't mentioned my goal? What did you think of it?'

She stuttered and stammered her response.

'Ah your goal . . . yes. Ah that . . . the thing is I . . . I kind of missed it. Yes, I missed it. I—'

'You missed it?'

'Yeah. Sorry. I . . . I was in the toilet.'

When you've got to go, and all that, I guess. In any case, the one I described to her in minute detail was far superior to the one I'd actually scored!

On that hot August day in 1985 when I made my way to Newcastle airport to meet her off the plane, nothing could spoil my happiness. Not my injured knee, and not my recently botched haircut that had left me with a mullet decidedly more green than blonde. My beautiful girlfriend was moving to Newcastle. My lonely days were over. My teammate and friend Neil McDonald drove me to the airport. We strode through the doors of the terminal modelling the finest clothes the city of Newcastle had to offer. We sported matching mullets, though his was definitely more blonde. We looked every inch the handsome, successful, professional footballers we were. I felt 10 feet tall. Invincible. Like I could fly. A group of young girls asked us for autographs as we waited for Geraldine to come through the double doors of the arrival hall. I was so excited as she did that I raced to greet her. It was a real moment. Time stood still. This was the moment we'd both been waiting for, the beginning of the rest of our lives together. I stared into her eyes and reached out my arms to embrace her. She didn't stare back into mine. She didn't embrace me. Instead her eyes were firmly fixed on the commotion over my left shoulder. It was like she was in a trance. Girls were screaming behind me. Geraldine finally spoke.

'Is that Spandau Ballet?'

I spun around and came face to chest with five rock stars, six foot tall and leather-clad, who strutted and smiled their way past me, and in doing so totally and utterly stole my moment. *Fucking Spandau Ballet!* Of all the people to rock up at Newcastle Airport in 1985, on the day you are really trying to impress your girlfriend, you don't want it to be fucking Spandau Ballet.

I eventually settled Geraldine down enough for us to leave the airport. The throng of screaming girls surrounded the band as we scuttled by.

Why couldn't she have been in the toilet and missed Spandau Ballet? If she had been, we wouldn't have had to talk about them all the way home in the car.

Home for our new life together was a recently rented flat. Geraldine's parents had only agreed to her moving on one condition – that she didn't live with me. The rented flat would've been a deal breaker for them. Not living together would have been unthinkable for us. We needed a charade to keep everyone happy. Every evening when Geraldine's parents rang 'my' flat, I'd set the phone down for five minutes while Geraldine and I sat beside it and waited. I'd then pick it up again.

'I can see her coming around the corner now. She'll be here any minute.'

Then we'd wait a little longer, before Geraldine would finally pick up the phone she'd been sitting beside for the whole time. We did that every night for a year. What nonsense!

But necessary nonsense. The joys of Catholicism.

Shearer - a Newcastle United Legend

There are Newcastle United fans. There are fanatical Newcastle United fans. Then there are legendary Newcastle United fans. 'Old Stevie' falls firmly into the last category. So, too, should John Shearer.

I met John on my first visit to St James' Park as a young player. He was a young man then too. He was standing outside the entrance of the old main stand, dressed head to toe in Newcastle United clothing adorned with a thousand pin badges. In all my 18-year association with the club I saw him every time I visited the stadium on match day. He was always dressed the same, always smiling, and never had a ticket to watch the game. When I could, I'd give him my complimentary tickets or any unused complimentary tickets that were lying around the changing room. Every time I did so, his face would crease into a broad smile. He'd thank me as if I'd given him £1 million.

During my time as a physio from 1993 to 2006, I'd give him my used training kit. Many a time I would meet him walking through town, proudly wearing the kit initialled PF. Years after leaving the club, I would go to a book talk, or a book signing, and the first person I'd meet would be John Shearer. I met him at one such signing in Waterstones in Newcastle in November 2024. I asked if he was there to buy my book. He shook his head.

'Nee way, man. I've just come to say hello to yee.'

I saw him once more on 14 December. It was late in the evening and I was taking my granddaughter, Isla, to the Northern Lights show at Leazes Park. John was walking out of St James' Park covered head to toe in Newcastle United clothing and memorabilia. Newcastle had beaten Leicester City 4-0 that afternoon. The final whistle had blown two hours previously. I suspect John had stood outside while the game took place, just out of his reach. I stopped to speak with him as always. He wasn't his cheery self, and said he wasn't feeling well. I offered to pay for an Uber to get him home. He refused, shook my hand, and wished me a Merry Christmas.

John died while I was preparing this manuscript. His passing didn't make the front or back pages, but there isn't a player or member of staff at Newcastle United over the past 40 years who didn't know John.

John Shearer – a Newcastle United Legend.

The old fashioned way to wish your fans a Happy New Year. Captain Glenn Roeder, on choreography, in January 1986.

'Divvent touch the soup...'

Newcastle United's punishment for being knocked out of the FA Cup in 1986 was to spend a week in Bermuda. We were required to play an exhibition game against Brian Clough's Nottingham Forest, but apart from that, it was a week on a paradise island, living in a luxury that I certainly wasn't accustomed to, training once or twice on the beach that hugged our hotel, and exploring the island's beauty and nightlife. Not a bad trade-off for failing to get past the third round of that year's FA Cup competition.

I was delighted to be included in the travelling party for the midseason jaunt. At the time I was right in the middle of a growing crisis with my ongoing knee problems. I was in a demoralising cycle of gruelling rehab, training for a week or two, breaking down, cortisone injection, gruelling rehab, training for a week or two, breaking down, cortisone injection – and repeat. Looking back now I can't fathom why the experienced surgeon who was overseeing my treatment didn't interject with an alternative plan. A surgical intervention maybe? I wasn't bold or brave enough to demand a second opinion, or to show any kind of displeasure about how my career-threatening and ultimately career-ending knee injury was being managed. I did get my surgery eventually – following a 17-month tailspin that began the day I'd wrecked my knee, and four months after I'd already been discarded by the club.

The Bermuda trip in January 1986 just happened to fall during one of the 'training again' periods of my shattering spiral towards footballing oblivion. My star was falling while my young teammate's was soaring. Perpetually excited and extremely talented, he was also on the plane to Bermuda. Paul Gascoigne was just beginning to make a name for himself for his football – while 'Gazza' was just beginning to make himself known for his mischief.

We arrived tired, and a little drunk, at the plush Elbow Beach Hotel Resort. It was a stunning location for our week on the island and remains one of the most luxurious hotels I have ever stayed in. The whole Newcastle United squad were taken on a tour of the opulent complex that was to be our home for the next seven days. We smiled and said hello to the many wealthy American guests welcoming this group of tracksuited footballers without any idea who they were. Our guide proudly ushered us towards the splendid pool area so that we could fully appreciate our sumptuous surroundings. We stopped by the side of the pool and the whole squad chatted to the holiday-makers there.

It wasn't apparent to any of us at first, but not quite the whole squad had stopped by the side of the pool. Without any warning, or any break in his stride, Gazza simply kept on walking. Then he started climbing. To the highest of the three diving boards that towered over the giant pool. He didn't stop there either. He just kept on walking, fully clothed. Right off the end of the board to plunge, fully clothed, into the crowded pool in front of the bemused hotel guests and his laughing teammates. He climbed out, didn't say a word, and joined on to the back of our group for the remainder of our tour. His trail of wet footprints snaking along the expensive hotel carpet were the only evidence that anything was amiss.

After checking in to my luxury beachfront chalet, I headed to the restaurant for some dinner. I met a disgruntled Gazza, who was coming out as I was going in. We stopped and chatted. He was still dripping wet from his dip in the pool. I asked him what the food was like and if he had any recommendations. He shook his head.

'The food's shite man. Divvent touch the soup whatever you do. Its fucking rank, man. There's fuck all in it.'

It was a pretty damning review for a five star hotel. I was a little surprised. As I sat down I still had high hopes for the food on offer. I would be avoiding the soup with fuck all in it, though. I scanned the menu as soon as it was handed to me. I might not be having the soup, but I wanted to see what ingredients were in it that had so agitated Gazza. The soup option was there. I asked the waiter what the French word in front of 'soup' meant. I'd never come across it before.

He described the dish on offer. Gazza had been right. There was fuck all in the soup: it was consommé. Clear soup.

Despite Gazza's warning, I had some after all. It was fucking rank. Gazza had been right about that as well. It tasted very different to the Heinz tomato soup dished up in working-class homes in Gazza's hometown of Dunston and in my hometown of Lisburn. You can take the boy out of . . .

One minute you're Steve McQueen . . .

The Bermuda trip was a bit of a bore and a chore for some of the older players in the squad; it was anything but for us younger members of the group. There were four of us: Neil McDonald and myself, both aged 20, and Paul Gascoigne and Paul Stephenson, both just 18. After a gentle training session on the beach in the mornings, we spent every afternoon riding around the paradise island on the motorbikes we'd hired from the hotel. It was a magical time in all of our young lives, riding in our swimming trunks, shirts off and without helmets. We'd stop at picture-perfect private beaches and swim in the warm water of the Atlantic. Then we'd climb back onto our bikes and let the wind blow-dry our bodies as we sped along the coastal route. I've never felt more alive and free than I did on those glory days hurtling along the deserted roads of that stunning island. We were just four boys having fun. With the wind in my mullet, and the warm air on my bare skin, I felt invincible. I felt like I was Steve McQueen. Admittedly, the engine on my bike sounded more like a hair dryer than the engine on Steve's machine when he jumped the first perimeter fence trying to make his great escape. But my bike ride did end the same way as his. I crashed!

One day, we stopped to chat to some of the senior players who were out for a walk. We were parked on the left side of the road, intending to double back on ourselves and make our way back to the hotel. My three companions turned their front wheels, crossed over into the opposite left lane and rode off behind me. I was finishing off my conversation with a couple of the senior players, turned my front wheel – and there was an almighty bang. I was knocked off my bike. But as I lay on the road, I watched in horror as the poor man, who'd crashed into my wheel, tumbled through the air. His bike was skidding along the road. Sparks were flying off it until it came to a standstill, 20 metres (65 feet) away from where I was trapped under my bike. The man finally made contact with the ground, then rolled and rolled before coming to a groaning standstill just in front of the wheels of a bus that'd screeched to a skidding halt as it came around the corner. He didn't move. *At all.* I thought he was dead. It was entirely my fault. I hadn't checked my mirror, or looked behind me before I'd turned my wheel. It was my fault alright. My mind raced. *He was dead. I was going to prison. My football career was over. My life was over.* I ignored the blood pouring down my thigh from where my skin used to be. I pushed my bike off me. I hobbled over to the victim of my stupidity. Some senior players had already reached him. He was screaming. At first, I thought he was screaming in pain. Then when I tried to pick up his bike, I realised he was screaming at us.

'Don't fucking touch me. Don't touch my fucking bike. Don't move a fucking thing until the police get here.'

The thought of the police coming made me sit down in the middle of the road. Made tears well in my eyes. Made my stomach heave. I'd knocked a man off his motorbike and he'd very nearly ended up under a bus. I looked at my thigh. The skin was completely ripped off it. I climbed back to my feet. I needed to apologise to my victim. I hobbled over to him and reached out my hand to him. He screamed at me.

'Don't touch me. Don't touch my fucking bike!'

I didn't touch him or his motorbike. I had no idea why I couldn't touch either. A siren was blaring as the car came to a stop, blocking off the middle of the road. Another police car pulled up behind the bus. I could hear radios and walkie-talkies, and there were flashing lights everywhere. This was it, I was getting thrown into prison, or off the island. I wiped my eyes with the back of my bloody hand. I was terrified. I needn't have been.

An officer approached me, smiling. He asked me what had happened. I told him that the accident was all my fault. I'd turned my wheel without checking my mirror or looking round. He left me sitting on the kerb and spent 10 minutes talking to the man lying on the road. Then he came back. 'That's us all sorted here. You can head back to your hotel and get cleaned up. Unless you would like me to take you to the local hospital?'

The man lying on the road got up. He lifted his motorbike. He climbed on and rode off. I told the officer I didn't understand what had just happened. He laughed.

'There is an enormous insurance claim culture here in Bermuda. The man is perfectly fine. He just wanted to ensure he would receive his claim.'

I chatted to the officer and his colleague for another 30 minutes. They were both from Nottingham, and they were both Nottingham Forest fans. They didn't have tickets for the game, so I invited them as my guests. They said it was OK for me to get back on my motorbike as long as it was still capable of transporting me back to my hotel. I didn't ride my bike back. I was too scared. Instead, I walked it all the way home. I've never ridden a motorbike since.

The officers came to the game. Their beloved Forest beat Newcastle United 3-0. I played with a heavy bandage on my thigh and my knee held up for a change. More importantly, I hadn't been sent to prison, or thrown off the island. Even more important than that, six months later I received a letter from Bermuda informing me the case was now officially closed and that the local man had received his compensation in full. It worked out well for everyone in the end.

Slipping out of the back door

In the past, when I was asked – and I was asked often – what it was like to have my football career ended prematurely by injury, I always used to reply that I just slipped out of the back door. It just seemed to me like one minute I was flying high: I was an integral part of the first team squad, part of Newcastle United, and I had a future in professional football. The next, I was down and out, no longer part of anything, and had no future in football whatsoever. It's only recently that the pain of losing the career I believed I was destined for has left me. Only now that the pain has gone am I able to revisit and re-evaluate those events that led to the end of my once promising career. Looking back, I know that I lost my career as a footballer predominantly because I simply didn't have the heart to fight hard enough to save it. For that, I'm angry with my younger, more subservient self – though I know that there were extenuating circumstances, which knocked me sideways and punched any fight I may have possessed clean out of me.

I never came close to recovering from the knee injury I sustained 14 months before Newcastle United ran out of patience. I was too accepting of the surgeon's suggestion that my injury wasn't serious enough to merit surgical intervention. I knew at the time that the injury was much more significant than he believed. He felt six weeks in a plaster cast would sort it. Four breakdowns, three cortisones and one year later, I should have been screaming from the rooftops that I wasn't happy with the management of my injury. But instead of questioning the eminent surgeon, I joined others at the club and questioned myself. I should have challenged the initial diagnosis and prognosis. I really should have challenged his insistence that the pain and instability I was experiencing every time I twisted, turned or tried to cross the ball was all inside my troubled head. Rather than dispute his assertions, I questioned myself instead. Maybe it *was* all in my head? Maybe I was too mentally weak?

Long before the management team engineered a way to remove me from the wage bill, I should have been strongly protesting that I had serious reservations about the surgeon's diagnosis and prognosis. I didn't say a word. I did nothing to help myself. I just did the rehab, broke down once more, had my latest jab – and on and on it would go. I should've read the large writing on the wall after my existing contract expired in June 1986. Rather than offer me a new one-year deal to replace the one I'd lost to my injury, the club placed me on a month-to-month contract. I didn't know it at the time, but professional clubs were prohibited from releasing injured players who'd come to the end of their contracts. They were, however, permitted to release injured players who came to the end of month-to-month deals. I was outmanoeuvred in a contract game I didn't even realise I was playing. I can see that painfully clearly now. On the day I left Newcastle United in October 1986, I still hadn't recovered from the injury I'd sustained in August 1985 – and I simply wasn't fit enough to attempt to resurrect my shattered career elsewhere.

I felt a real sense of injustice at how I'd been treated. I was angry, I was ready for the fight. I wasn't going to let myself be discarded like that. I called the Professional Footballers' Association. They found me another surgeon, who scheduled me for surgery that he hoped might fix the problem. I wasn't finished with Newcastle United either. The day I left the club the manager, Willie McFaul, told me to call him if I ever needed anything. I did need something. I needed help to save my career. I called his office on three occasions. Each time the secretary said she'd pass the message on. I never got a reply. I was angrier still, full of fight.

I underwent my surgery in January 1987 with high hopes that it would be a success. I was up for the battle back to fitness and back into professional football. Then on 3 February, 1987, the world as I'd known it came to an end. My beautiful but frail mother, Bernadette, died suddenly from a heart attack. My fight for my career died with her. I did my rehab, but my heart was with my mother. Six months later, it became obvious that despite the surgeon's best attempts, my knee would remain too unstable for me ever to return to professional football.

In those dark days of 1986/87, my world had simply fallen apart. I'd slipped out of the back door of the career I'd been destined to pursue since the day I first kicked a ball.

Thankfully, life doesn't always move in the direction we think it is going. It takes us places we never expect to go. My life took me all the way back to Newcastle United . . .

Walking through the front door

It was October 1993. I was working as a newly qualified physiotherapist at the Freeman Hospital in Newcastle. It had been seven years since my professional playing career had ended. I'd carried on playing part-time football for a little while, mainly because I needed the money to support us through some bleak times when the only income we had was from Geraldine's role as a sales assistant at Northern Electric and the small amount I provided from my student loan.

I had not once harboured thoughts or dreams of returning to the club. Why would I? I was hurt and bitter about how easily the club had thrown me away. Football was a harsh world that was better left in the past. I'd enjoyed my time as a student, was proud of my achievement of graduating as a physiotherapist and I was loving my first job at the Freeman. Life was good again. I was back in the world of work, after seven years of striving to get there. My ambition was to work my way up the physiotherapy ladder in the Health Service. Then, one October day, while I was kneeling behind a stroke patient working with her to try to reduce the spasm in her left arm, a colleague informed me that there was someone on the phone. I told him I was a little busy with my patient, asked if he could take a message and to tell the caller I would call back. Then I asked him who the caller was. I nearly dropped my patient when he told me.

'It's Derek Wright from Newcastle United. I'll tell him you'll call back.'

I could feel a thump in my chest. *Derek Wright? Newcastle United?* I hadn't spoken to my former physiotherapist since the day I'd left seven years previously. It's not that I hadn't wanted to; I had. On many occasions too. I'd always got on well with Derek. He was a genuine man and when I was enduring the torturous struggles with my knee, I regarded him as a friend. I hadn't contacted him, or anyone from the club for that matter, purely because I was too embarrassed. I didn't want any of them to think I was hanging around like a bad smell. I think I was also burying the hurt of losing my career.

Now, only months after I had qualified as a physiotherapist, Derek Wright, from Newcastle United, was calling the Freeman Hospital, to speak with me. I knew what that call meant. So too did my thumping chest. I sat my patient down as gently as my excited arms would permit, chased my colleague along the hallway to the reception desk and snatched the phone, a little too forcefully, from his hand.

Taking that call took me all the way back to Newcastle United. It took me home.

I was back at Newcastle United by the beginning of November 1993. I would remain as a physiotherapist there for the following 13 years. Walking back into Newcastle United that day remains one of the proudest moments of my life. Everything about the club had changed since I'd departed in 1986. The stadium had been transformed, Kevin Keegan had returned and breathed new life into the club and the city, and the inadequate old training facility at Benwell had been consigned to history. All was so utterly altered that I got lost on my way to the training ground at Maiden Castle, Durham. I was wandering aimlessly along the river towpath for 10 minutes before I spotted some roofers working on a derelict house. I called out to them to ask for directions to Newcastle United's training facility. One of them pointed up ahead.

'Just follow the smell of the shite!'

In my excitement, I'd forgotten that Durham City was home to Sunderland supporters too. Walking proudly through the front door of the football club that had shipped me out of the back door seven years previously was an assault on my senses. I felt like I was floating.

That's one way to stand out from the crowd. Gallowgate End v Tottenham Hotspur in 1986. I hope it was a warm day.

I was having conversations with Kevin Keegan and the rest of the staff, but not really paying attention to the detail of what anyone was saying. My mind wouldn't let me settle; was just buzzing.

I'd spent barely an hour in the treatment room, meeting with players and staff, before my lack of concentration nearly ended in disaster. I was working with Lee Clark, strapping his leg into the isokinetic equipment that the club had purchased only weeks before. Derek had shown me how to use it, but my mind just wasn't computing. It began computing again only when I trapped my thumb between Lee Clark's leg and the harsh metal of the machinery. I screamed in pain. Lee screamed for help. After lot of shouting, bleeding and embarrassment on my part, Derek Wright ran into the treatment room and hit the emergency stop button. I, my crushed thumb, and my embarrassment, were free once again. It was a somewhat inauspicious start.

Derek bandaged my thumb and gave me a drink of water. I lay on the treatment couch. Players and staff shuffled in and out of the room. The conversation was familiar; I'd heard it all before. I felt my eyes sting. I hadn't realised how much I'd missed it. I wiped a tear with my bandaged thumb. I was home once more.

'I thought you drove an Aston Martin?'

Football had changed dramatically since it had left me behind in 1986. It was awash with money. The birth of the Premier League, and the influx of millions of pounds from Sky TV, meant that the Newcastle United I rejoined as a physiotherapist bore little resemblance to the club where I'd worked as a young player. Money was the driver.

Back in 1986, my salary was £175 a week. The top earners at the club would be on £1,000, with one or two on a little more than that. Between 1986 and 1993, we'd been living on the proceeds of my student loan and Geraldine's earnings from her job as a sales assistant. When I returned to the club, we were still living in the same cramped flat we'd bought just before I commenced my university course. Our car was a 10-year-old Renault 5. Geraldine drove it; I hadn't yet passed my driving test.

In my first few months back at the club, I travelled to the training ground in Durham via bus and train. Occasionally I'd cadge a lift from the kitman, Ray Thompson, in his crammed white van. In the mornings I'd walk the short distance from the bus stop on the main road to our base within the university playing fields. Every day there would be a steady stream of supercars cruising past me before they parked up in a shiny expensive row along the edge of the training pitches. With money comes flash cars. In 1993, I had neither money nor a flash car. Barry Venison had both. He was also suffering from persistent back problems during my early days and weeks back at the club. The vast chasm, between the high-earning footballer and the struggling physiotherapist, was never more in evidence than on the day I attempted to get to the bottom of Barry Venison's back problems.

Barry was a very likeable, intelligent, engaging man. He was also one of the flashier characters I met in my first days back at the club. He sported a perfectly coiffured blonde mullet, wore designer clothes to training every day, and was dripping in expensive jewellery.

'I THOUGHT YOU DROVE AN ASTON MARTIN?'

We were in the busy treatment room. I was scratching around searching for the possible cause of the stiffness in his back. I recalled seeing him driving into training that morning in his sporty supercar.

'Maybe your car is causing it? What make is it?'

'It's a DB7.'

I was a little confused and raised an eyebrow.

'Oh, right. I thought you drove an Aston Martin?'

The whole treatment room laughed as Barry shook his head.

'A DB7 *is* an Aston Martin, you nugget!'

I raised my palms to the room. I was operating in an alien world. I hadn't seen many Aston Martins in our council estate in Lisburn, the streets of Denton Burn, or on my university campus in Longbenton. When the laughter subsided, I vowed to brush up on my knowledge of supercars. I needed to if I wished to thrive and survive in my new surroundings.

Barry got rid of his DB7, and his back issue resolved itself within days. He thanked me for my help. I may not have known my cars, but I did know my ergonomics.

The great Arthur Cox with the always smiling Barry Venison. Two good men who did brilliant jobs for Newcastle United.

The Kevin Keegan effect - 1992-97

It is a rare thing when a single player not only completely transforms a football club, but also impacts an entire city and region. Kevin Keegan did just that in his short spell as a player between 1982 and 1984. When he returned to the club in 1992 as an untried and untested manager, the club was once again in dire straits. Facing the ignominy of being relegated to the third tier of English football for the first time, the board of directors reached out more in desperation than hope to a man who could, at the very least, galvanise players and fans alike. It proved to be one of the most inspired appointments in the entire history of Newcastle United.

Kevin Keegan, the manager, made an even greater impression on the club and on the city than he had done a decade before. Relegation was avoided, promotion was achieved the following season and his team finished third in its first season back in the top flight in 1993/94. He came within a whisker of winning the Premier League in his last full season in 1995/96, before his surprise departure in January 1997. Amazingly, he did all of that while his team played a brand of swashbuckling, free-flowing, attacking football rarely seen before or since. He returned to the club for an ill-fated spell under the Ashley regime, but that did nothing to tarnish his reputation. If anything, the dignity he showed at that time served only to cement his legacy in the north-east.

Kevin Keegan spent less than seven seasons in total with Newcastle United – and left an imprint that will last for generations. It was a privilege to have had a front row seat. My boyhood idol didn't disappoint. A statue maybe?

'She *is* looking at him!'

I'd barely opened the door to the coaches' changing room. Kevin Keegan was on the phone and clearly agitated. He hung up and pointed in my direction,

'You go and get him out of that hospital before the press get wind of him being there.'

He was ushering me out of the room as he outlined my mission.

I'd been back at the club for only a matter of weeks. I was happy to follow Kevin's orders and prove myself to be a good addition to his backroom staff. I had only the one problem: I hadn't yet passed my driving test. I couldn't just go to the hospital and get whoever was in there out of there before the press found out. Kevin scanned the coaches' room for a driver. Five minutes later, my friend John Carver, the youth team coach at the time, was driving me to the hospital.

John gave me a little bit of background on the player we were on our way to extract. He had been having problems at home and at work. Like many before him, and many since, he had tried to find a fix at the bottom of a bottle. These attempts at a solution had only exacerbated his woes at home, and had most probably cost him his career at Newcastle United. He'd ended up in hospital that morning after a very heavy night of drinking.

As John parked up outside the infirmary, I was a little apprehensive. I had no idea what might confront us or how we might deal with it. As we walked towards the ward, it was obvious that John Carver was also uncomfortable about this undercover mission to extract our asset. His cap was pulled down over his eyes, and those eyes were hidden firmly behind the biggest pair of sunglasses I'd ever seen. He was glancing from left to right, avoiding all eye contact with the doctors and nurses who smiled at us as we passed them by. He was also walking on tiptoes. I grabbed his arm. He jumped.

'You alright? What the fuck are you walking like that for?'

He was a little offended.

'Walking like what?'

I demonstrated to him how he had been walking. He wasn't convinced.

'Fuck off, man. I'm not walking like that.'

We agreed to differ. I began walking towards the ward. John walked beside me in exactly the same way as before. I stopped and looked at him. He took his dark glasses off and threw his arms wide.

'What, man? Leave me alone. I fucking hate these places. Let's just get on with it and get out of here.'

I did what he asked and let the world's worst undercover agent tiptoe alongside me all the way to the ward.

Our stricken player was a very sorry sight to see. He was in a corner bed of four. His three roommates were all over 70 years old, and our player looked older than any of them. He had a tube in his nose and lines in both wrists. He turned his yellowy eyes in our direction. He got extremely agitated when he recognised us, and began thrashing around. John, in his cap and dark glasses, tiptoed around the far side of the bed. I sat down and took the player's hand. He squeezed so hard on mine that I wished I hadn't offered it to him in the first place. I tried to calm him down. I told him we were there to take him home as soon as the doctor in charge of his care was happy to release him. He tightened his grip and pulled himself up the bed as he spoke.

'Thank fuck you're here. They're trying to kill me. They're all from the estate. They've got guns, knives, the lot. You have to help me. You've to get me out of here now. Get me out of here. Get me out of this place.'

He was making no sense. His levels of paranoia were off the scale. I'd never seen that level of paranoia in anyone before and I've never seen it since. It was terrifying to witness. I hid my shock. He didn't need a flustered, out-of-his-depth physio, he needed a composed, in-control friend. I rubbed his hand.

'There's no one out to get you. You've had a bit of a bad time, but you're in the right place. These people are trying to look after you.'

My fake calmness and fake confidence seemed to do the trick. He stopped fidgeting and released the vice on my hand. I rubbed it to encourage some blood flow back into my white knuckles. He settled back in the bed and his breathing slowed. Then he looked over my shoulder. He dug his nails into my forearm. I turned to observe the smiling ward sister who'd entered the room. She was tending to the old man diagonally across from us. She was chatting with her patient, laughing with his family, and paying no attention whatsoever to our drama in the other corner. Our paranoid player, though, was interpreting the harmless scene very differently to how it was actually playing out, and his sharp nails were drawing blood from my arm. He was shouting at me in a whisper.

'Her. Her there. She's fucking looking at me. She's the one. She's the ringleader. Look. Look at her. She's fucking eyeing me up. She's trying to kill me. She's looking at me.'

I unclipped his nails from my bleeding arm and attempted to reassure him as before. I recruited John for help this time.

'John, will you please assure him that she is not looking at him, or trying to kill him.'

John lowered his shades. He glanced at me, he glanced at the ward sister, and he glanced at our paranoid player. Then he said,

'She *is* looking at him!'

Jesus Christ! Talk about not helping!

Our paranoid player began thrashing around the bed. He screamed and shouted obscenities. He pulled on his tubes and lines. He tried to jump out of his bed. It took three members of staff to restrain him!

We did eventually get him home that afternoon. The press were none the wiser.

I'm not sure when Agent Carver took his cap and glasses off. He was still wearing them when we parted company. He did not accompany me on further undercover missions.

The Young Ones

Kevin Keegan's fantastic team of the mid '90s was packed full of brilliant footballers whose names easily roll off the tongue today. Shearer, Beardsley, Ferdinand, Ginola, Gillespie, Asprilla, Albert, Lee, Batty – each and every one richly deserves every accolade they receive for playing a vital part in one of the most fabled teams in Newcastle United's history. They may not have matched the Cup wins and League titles of Moncur, Milburn and Gallacher, but they came agonisingly close. They gave all of us who were lucky enough to be there some of the best footballing memories of our lives.

There were another group of players, though, who played an enormous part in Kevin's revolution. A band of brothers who'd come through the youth system together in darker times. Once exposed to the bright light of Kevin Keegan's revolution, they morphed into outstanding footballers, capable not only of holding their own among the newly arrived superstars, but of positively thriving in their new environment. As a young player who'd made my way through the youth system at Newcastle United only to have my career ended abruptly, I felt immense pride in watching the development of Steve Howey, Lee Clark, Steve Watson and Robbie Elliott. Each and every one of them made a significant contribution to the success of Kevin's illustrious team. Steve Howey, rightly became an international footballer. The other three were worthy of that honour too. They were grounded and humble, and it was a genuine pleasure to work with them. Well done, the Young Ones.

'D'you wanna go for a drink?'

The paranoid player from hospital just couldn't seem to put his troubles behind him. It was unsurprising; his marriage was failing. From my conversations with the club surgeon, it was equally obvious his career was likely to be prematurely curtailed because of injury. I could certainly sympathise with the pain of losing a football career.

Life at a football club goes on all around you when you're injured. You're still part of the group. You're invited on all of the nights out. You turn up at the training ground every day, just like all of your teammates. But then training starts and you're no longer taking part. As your colleagues jog the training pitch, you walk to the treatment room. When your friends finish their lunch and drive home, you trudge back to the treatment room for your afternoon session. When the big match comes around and your teammates file into the home dressing room, you make your way to the stands, and there's a spectacle that you were born to be part of and you're just a spectator. You become the invisible man.

The life of the long-term injured footballer is a lonely one. Add a marriage breakdown, and problems with alcohol, and the clock to inevitable self-destruction begins ticking a little louder and a little faster. Two days after the hospital incident, the troubled player arrived at the training ground carrying a holdall. Nothing unusual about that. On this occasion, there was everything unusual. He told a teammate he had a shotgun in his bag! He needed it to protect himself from the people who were trying to kill him. It was an unsettling moment for his confidant, who approached a member of staff. Within minutes the matter was resolved when a search of the bag revealed nothing other than a change of clothes and a washbag. Looking back now it seems to me incredible that nothing was done to help such an obviously troubled human being. But nothing was. Instead, he reported to the training ground every day. He was on time, he dedicated himself to his rehab, and he stank of alcohol. Every single day.

In an attempt to help him with his injury, an appointment was made for him to attend the local university for an assessment, using a high-tech piece of testing equipment it had recently purchased. I arrived early for the test, but our player staggered in an hour late, reeking of alcohol. The professor, who'd given up his time for us, shook his head as he left us there in the lab room. His junior colleague carried on as best he could, but his efforts were pointless. The assessment had to be aborted, as our player was in no fit state to carry on. I was embarrassed – for him and for me. It was a shockingly unprofessional sight.

Embarrassment wasn't my biggest concern, though. I was seriously worried for his well-being – especially after what I'd witnessed in the hospital a month before. Forget football; he was some girl's husband, some mother's son, and some child's father. He was totally lost and nobody seemed to care. I had no idea what to do to help. I just knew that I had to do something. I wanted to get to the underlying cause of his drinking, or whatever else he was doing. Maybe then I could point him in the right direction to help him get his life back on track.

It was early afternoon. We were about to go our separate ways after the debacle of the university appointment. He had sobered up. He shook my hand and apologised for his performance at the lab. I felt like I couldn't just let him leave to continue his cycle of destruction. I had to intervene. I had to get him to open up to me. Only then could I possibly hope to help him. I hatched a plan on the spot.

'Do you fancy going for a drink?'

Possibly, on reflection, that wasn't the smartest suggestion to make to someone I suspected was dealing with serious alcohol issues. He, of course, said yes immediately.

I took him to a city centre bar I'd frequented several times, and where I knew the management. It was quiet when we arrived. We spent all afternoon there. No matter how hard I probed my troubled player, he never once opened up about his issues. Instead, he showed me, and the other customers, his full repertoire of party tricks. He interspersed the tricks with anecdote after anecdote from his playing and drinking career. He was brilliant company and provided hours of entertainment. Evening fell, and the half-empty afternoon bar was now alive with people. The manager approached me.

'Paul. It was OK earlier 'cos the bar was quiet, but people are starting to complain about the noise and the language.'

I tried to reassure her, without drawing the attention of my troubled footballer. I whispered to her.

'He has a few issues. I'll try to calm him down. Don't worry, I'll sort it.'

She shook her head.

'No, Paul. You don't understand. They're not complaining about him. They're complaining about you!'

Bloody hell.

My troubled player had gotten me so drunk, I could barely stand up straight. I paid my bill and sheepishly slipped out of the bar. I peered through the window. My troubled player was holding court right in the centre of the new venue I had introduced him to. It became his nightly haunt until he was eventually shipped out to become some other club's problem.

That was my last ever attempt at counselling. I concentrated on physiotherapy after that. The player's career ended shortly after he left, as did his marriage. I don't believe he ever got over his alcohol issues.

A Newcastle United family

Ray Thompson is a name that is not readily known to all but the most diehard Newcastle United followers. Yet this immensely likeable and hard-working character has been an important and popular staff member for over 35 years. Part of the stadium maintenance team from 1988 to 1993, he switched roles to become the Kitman under Kevin Keegan. I met him on my first day back as a physiotherapist. I quickly learned he was a man of great integrity, with an outstanding work ethic and unbreakable loyalty to Newcastle United. He became a trusted friend and confidant, and remains so to this day.

Many things have changed for Ray over the years. Unfortunately, his haircut has remained the same during that entire period. I often wonder how that is even possible. His life, though, has changed in so many ways thanks to Newcastle United. He met his lovely wife Phillipa, when she too was working at the club. And his son Max is now a very promising goalkeeper and regular member of the first team squad. Max has been on the club's books since he was 11 years old. He has already played in the Football League for both Northampton Town and Chesterfield. Should the special day ever arrive when he stands between the posts at St James' Park representing his hometown club, what a magical moment it will be, not just for Max, but for an amazing family made at Newcastle United. You never know, Ray might even change his hairstyle to mark the occasion. I doubt it, though.

The bell rings for round one

The professional football environment is unique. A workplace like no other. It throws up situations and generates characters who live long in the memory. In every one of my 18 seasons at Newcastle United, the same unofficial roles were played by several different characters. The faces changed, the names changed, but the roles remained. Vacant for a short while after the departure of the previous incumbent, but never remaining unoccupied for long.

Some roles were given whether the recipient wanted them or not. Others were fought over and had to be earned. There were the obvious, coveted roles – team captain, club captain, players' committee member. Then there were the more idiosyncratic roles. The events organiser, the dressing room 'dunce' and the team 'character', The events organiser was usually an older, sensible member of the group, someone who'd been around the block and back again. He understood just how important extracurricular activities were for building team togetherness and camaraderie. He would suggest various events to bring the families together and he might organise the Christmas party or the end-of-season trip abroad. He was well intentioned, well organised and well respected, and he earned his title through doing. Over time it was obvious to the others, who couldn't be bothered to organise anything, exactly who the best person for the job was. He was the only one who bothered his arse to arrange the team's social schedule.

The team dunce never really knew he was that. Everyone else in the building most certainly did. It's often assumed that professional footballers are not the brightest individuals in the community. I have met many supremely intelligent footballers during my time in the game, but it's true that football isn't a hotbed of intellectualism. Most footballers are poorly educated academically for obvious reasons: they're in full-time employment as footballers from the age of 16 and, in the 10 years prior to taking up that employment, they're dedicating every waking hour to trying to become the next George Best, Kevin Keegan or Harry Kane. Having pointed that out, I can say that most footballers operate at a certain level of intelligence. What they may lack in formal education, they more than make up for by being streetwise. What I'm trying to say is that I disagree with the old adage that all footballers are thick. Most aren't, though it is very obvious that some most certainly are. It is from this pool that the team 'dunce' emerges. He is the player that even the thick players regard as thick. Over my entire 18 years in football there was always someone at the club who would leave me scratching my head as to how he ever got through an education system.

The team 'character' reveals himself. Football is full of jokers, wisecracks and comedians. A happy changing room at a professional football club is a magnificent place to be. It is filled with laughter, sledging, good nature and fun. It is not the place for the faint of heart or those of a sensitive disposition. Jokes are ten a penny, pranks are a daily occurrence and biting comments fly through the air as quickly as the laughter that follows them. There are many worthy contenders for the role of team 'character', but in my experience there is always one individual who emerges as the cock of the walk. He is the one with the best jokes, the sharpest tongue, the most outrageous pranks. He goes the extra mile to entertain the group at all times. He is hugely popular and he revels in his role. This character plays a vital role at the club: he lifts the mood after a defeat and he leads the charge after a win.

The Newcastle United I joined as a physio in 1993 was full of characters, but one man stood head and shoulders above the rest. That man was Malcolm Allen. Malcolm was a Welsh international centre-forward. He told me a joke on my first day in the treatment room. I laughed, so he told me another 10 before he left the room. I can think now of so many examples of him bringing the house down with his latest one-liner or ridiculous prank. He was a joy to work with and a pleasure to be around. He provided so many laughs that it is a struggle to pick out one example from all of the others.

One of my favourite moments occurred when we travelled to Coventry for a reserve game. Jeff Clarke, our reserve team coach, was delivering his final instructions to the team. Malcolm Allen was sitting just on the periphery of Jeff's vision. He looked a picture of concentration. He was staring into space, seemingly hanging on every one of his earnest coach's words of wisdom. Jeff wasn't quite finished when the bell rang in the changing room to notify us it that it was time to make our way onto the pitch. As Jeff ignored the bell and continued with his team talk, Malcolm Allen sprang to his feet behind him. He proceeded to skip and box his way around his imaginary ring like he was taking part in round one of a crucial world title fight. Malcolm sat back down again just as Jeff turned to see why the changing room was now convulsed with laughter. He looked at Malcolm, who sat staring into space as if nothing untoward had occurred. It was a brilliant moment from a wonderful character.

Malcolm Allen's career ended far too prematurely through injury. Of those who had the privilege of working with him, I won't be the only person to remember with fondness his many great performances both on and off the pitch.

The weigh-in, scissors and a trip to the post office

There was one young apprentice footballer in 1994 who provided us with unintended entertainment every day when he visited our treatment room. He was naturally funny, a bit of a joker, but also the least intelligent footballer I've ever met. From the moment he first walked through the treatment room door, to the day he was released by the club, I looked forward to my daily interactions. Some of the things he said, and some of the things he did, were so ridiculous that I initially thought he was having a laugh at my expense. Never before or since have I had genuine concerns about how a particular individual managed to make his way through a day, never mind cope with the challenges life throws at us all. I couldn't help but like him, but I couldn't help but worry for him either.

One memorable morning I was standing at the side of the measuring scales as he approached them wearing just a towel. He was having his preseason weigh-in to check that he'd been looking after himself during the summer break. We exchanged pleasantries and he was keen to tell me how hard he'd been working out during the off season. He said he'd been eating well and he felt he was in the best shape of his life. He fully expected to be a pound or two lighter than he was when he'd departed at the end of the previous season. He climbed onto the scales, still wearing his towel. I balanced the weights. I shook my head and informed him that he was three pounds overweight. That would mean a small fine for reporting back overweight. He was distraught.

'That can't be right, man. I've been training all summer. I haven't even so much as looked at a beer, or sniffed a bar of Cadbury's Diary Milk, man. Your scales must be broken.'

He was nearly crying by the time he'd finished talking. I felt very sorry for him. I wanted to help him make the weight.

'Why don't you take your towel off? That will maybe account for

What a time to be at Newcastle United. I didn't fully appreciate it back then, but I now regard it as the privilege of my life to have been a very small part of it.

the extra two or three pounds? It might save you having to pay a fine.'

He was grateful for my help.

He removed his towel just as I'd suggested. The scales didn't move. He was devastated.

'It's still the fucking same, man! Oh for fuck's sake! That's a fine for me!'

I began to laugh. He didn't appreciate that I wasn't taking the matter seriously.

'It's no laughing matter, man. I've worked my bollox off all summer. Now I'm going to have to pay a fine I can't afford and all you can do is laugh!'

I stopped laughing and gave him my best professional straight face as I spoke.

'I think it might make all the difference to your weight readings on the scales if you actually let go of the towel you're holding in the air!'

It took a minute or two of explaining, but he eventually set the towel on the floor. He punched the air as the scales reacted to its removal. He had avoided the fine! He smiled to himself as he made his way up the corridor. I'm still not convinced he ever understood why setting the towel on the ground made any difference.

Another time, he came into the treatment room with a pair of new boots in his hand.

'Can I borrow your scissors?'

I handed them to him. He took his boots over to the adjacent treatment couch. I studied him as he held up the laces of his boot so they were standing vertically in the air. He squinted as he raised his scissors. He expertly cut the longer lace. He pulled the laces back into the air. He squinted at them again. He then cut the longer one to match the other. He repeated the process three times more, before he was happy to move on to his other boot. I intervened at that point.

'What are you doing?'

He ignored me, squinted at his laces and cut the longer one. He responded as he was raising his laces once more. One eye was closed as he spoke, without taking the other eye off his troublesome laces.

'What do you think I'm doing, man? I'm trying to get these fucking laces the same length. They're right bastards, though. I keep cutting one shorter than the other. There'll be no laces left by the time I'm done.'

I walked over to where he was squinting and cutting. Much to his distress, I calmly took the boot and scissors from him. He was astonished when I pulled the laces through the boot until they were the same length. He looked at me like I was Albert Einstein himself.

'Fuck me. You're so clever, man. That's unbelievable.'

As he left the treatment room with his matching laces, and new-found skills, I couldn't help but agree with him. It was unbelievable.

Still, he was aware he wasn't the brightest of individuals, and he was more than happy to laugh at himself. He came rushing into the treatment room one morning. He couldn't wait to tell me, and everyone else in there, how he'd queued in the post office for 30 minutes the day before. When he'd reached the front of the lengthy queue, he'd asked the girl behind the counter for a book of four stamps. He was taken aback when she'd bluntly refused his perfectly reasonable request.'

'Why not?'

He said the girl smiled back at him as she pointed to her left.

'Because this is Barclay's Bank. The post office is two doors down.'

He was a one-off. I missed him when he left. He drifted out of football and I don't know what became of him. I sincerely hope he picked up some life skills along his journey.

Maiden Castle

By the mid '90s, St James' Park had changed beyond all recognition from the one I'd experienced the decade before. The new all-seater stadium was a magnificent upgrade from the dilapidated old one of the '80s. The main stand now was the brand-new Jackie Milburn Stand; the rump of the Leazes End was the Sir John Hall Stand (although it will always be the Leazes); the Gallowgate End was the South Stand (although it will always be the Gallowgate). Only the East Stand, built in the '70s, remained. The Milburn and The Leazes stands would undergo further development: through a remarkable feat of engineering, a new tier was added to both without hindrance to the regular attendance figures during construction. The giant stadium towered over the city like never before, visible for miles around. If anyone doubted Newcastle was a football city, they'd be put right when approaching from any direction. This city was the home of Newcastle United, and Newcastle United was a formidable force in football once more.

The training ground facilities were also unrecognisable. We had moved. We had improved. Run-down Benwell was consigned to the history books. Kevin Keegan had insisted on a relocation to Maiden Castle in Durham City, if the club ever hoped to attract the calibre of player he had in mind. Maiden Castle was an upgrade on Benwell, no doubt, but it was also the sports complex for Durham University. So it was a regular occurrence for the superstar footballers from Newcastle

United to be standing naked in the showers alongside starstruck students from the university sports teams. The indoor facilities were better than Benwell, but they weren't spectacular by any means. The pitches were pristine, though, and that was the most important thing.

On a quiet morning, it was a regular treat for me to watch some of the most talented players in the country go hell for leather at each other in the most fiercely contested five-a-side games I've ever seen. When I say I saw the games, I mean I had a partial view. I was often obstructed by hordes of fans, standing five or six rows deep, enjoying their burgers and hotdogs from the nearby burger van. Kevin Keegan made the decision to welcome fans to watch training sessions. Sometimes, as many as 5,000 a day took him up on his offer. It was an inspired move and I think it only served to strengthen the unique bond forged by the players with their devoted fans.

Poulet à la compote, a strapping and a grumpy Belgian

The great Billy Bingham was honoured with a well-deserved testimonial on 12 August, 1994. He had played with distinction for his country, before leading it to two consecutive World Cup tournaments in 1982 and 1986.

I had come tantalisingly close to making the 1982 squad. I'd made my debut for Newcastle United as a 16-year-old in the May just before the final squad was announced. I received a phone call from Billy before the announcement informing me just how close I'd come to making his squad, and he promised to include me in the next training camp following the finals. He was true to his word, and I was part of his first training camp following the team's remarkable success in Spain. Sadly, that was as close as I ever got to a full international call-up, before injury ended my career. I spoke with Billy Bingham on several occasions during that injury-ravaged spell. He never gave up on me. He brought me to Under 21 get-togethers during the summer holidays. I spent my time with the physio while the fit players enjoyed their sessions in the sun. It was demoralising but uplifting at the same time to know I was in Billy's thoughts through dark times. I am grateful to him for that.

After my career ended, I spent seven years cut adrift from the professional game before returning as a physiotherapist. I had been back in the professional game for only a matter of months when the Billy Bingham testimonial came around in August 1994. After returning to the club the previous October, I was very much regarded as the junior physiotherapist. I would work all week in the treatment room alongside my more experienced colleague Derek Wright, but when it came to away games or away trips, I was left behind to tend to the injured players. I missed out on the anticipation, excitement and thrills of the match-day atmosphere.

The Billy Bingham testimonial was a significant day for me because it was the first professional game where I was the sole physiotherapist for the Newcastle United first team. Kevin Keegan had decided it would be a nice treat for me to travel to Northern Ireland with the team. He was right. I was so proud to be going home as a small part of Newcastle United again. After all, the club was the reason I had left the country of my birth in the first place. I was very excited, but I was a little nervous too. I really wanted to impress Kevin and the senior players on my first trip, and in my first game, as a physio.

The team was flying high, and had finished the season in third place in the Premier League on its first season out of the Championship. It was clear to everyone that Newcastle United was back and on the rise again. That third-place finish ensured Kevin was in a position to add quality players to his overachieving squad. He'd spent the summer commentating on the World Cup in the USA, which had given him a perfect opportunity to assess the best players the world had to offer. It was no surprise, then, when Newcastle United swooped for the hugely impressive Belgian international Philippe Albert. He joined the club just prior to the trip to Belfast.

Philippe arrived with an enormous reputation, courtesy of his outstanding performances at the World Cup. Everyone at the club was excited by his signing. It seemed to represent the beginning of a new era. Only a year before, Newcastle United had been a second division club. Only two years before, it had very nearly been a third division club. Now it was signing one of the top players in the world. This was, without a doubt, a statement of intent.

In those days, the physio was in charge of taking the players' food orders for prematch meals. I hadn't spoken a word to our new superstar signing since he'd joined the club. I made my way nervously to his hotel room to ascertain his requirements. I knocked on the door. He opened it so fast that I thought he must have been standing behind it waiting for my knock. I stepped back in fright. This giant of a man stood, sour-faced, in front of me, blocking all of the light from the window behind him. I introduced myself as he cast his shadow over me. I asked what he wanted to eat for his prematch meal. His reply was delivered bluntly.

'Poulet à la compote.'

I stared blankly at him and then at my notepad. I asked him again. He repeated his order. I had no idea what he was saying.

I hadn't learned much French at St Patrick's. I searched my brain, and remembered that *poulet* had to mean 'chicken', but had I no idea what the *compote* was. Jam, maybe? Philippe got very agitated when I suggested it might be jam. I started sweating and made a couple more stabs at it with no success. By the time I left his door, he was shaking his head and throwing his arms in the air in exasperation. I was hot, sweaty and embarrassed that I hadn't been able to work out what our grumpy new superstar usually ate for his prematch meal. I didn't want to admit defeat in front of Kevin Keegan and the players, so I made my way to the hotel kitchen. The chef solved the problem in seconds. Philippe Albert got his unusual prematch combination of chicken and apple sauce. I vowed to brush up on my French.

In the changing room before the game I was nervous. I was confident too, though. I had done brilliantly at university and had taken my new role in professional football in my stride. I knew I was more than competent as a physiotherapist. I'd just completed an advanced taping and strapping course, as part of my transitioning from working in the hospital setting to now working with professional footballers. Philippe Albert, with his belly full of chicken and apple sauce, asked me if I would strap his ankle. I was delighted. Here was a chance to redeem myself. With Kevin Keegan looking over my shoulder, I applied the strapping perfectly, just as I'd been taught on my recent course. Kevin nodded approvingly. It was a thing of beauty.

I got up to work my art on my next ankle. I made eye contact with Philippe, waiting for the inevitable nod of approval for what must have been one of the best ankle strappings he'd ever had applied to his expensive leg. He didn't make eye contact, but instead began shaking his head and ripping my perfection off his fussy ankle. I was more than a little flustered as I tried again. He ripped my efforts off again. I began sweating like I'd already played 90 minutes in Billy Bingham's testimonial. Kevin Keegan was back asking what the problem was. Two or three of the players were enjoying my pain and enquiring as to whether or not I'd actually learned how to strap an ankle at university. Some were telling me to give Derek Wright a ring and see if he could get a flight over and help me out. Bastards . . . but funny bastards with it. Philippe dismissed me with a wave of his hand. He took a strapping from the table and did it himself. I was mortified.

The game commenced but I couldn't concentrate. Thoughts of chicken and apple sauce, thoughts of strappings, thoughts of never being asked to come on another trip, danced around my head for most of the match. Then George Best entered the field of play. He was so obviously drunk that it was both shocking and sad. Contemplating the sadness of what I was witnessing finally banished Philippe Albert from my mind.

When I got back to the hotel, I called my colleague Derek Wright. I told him all about the compote, the strapping and the grumpy superstar we'd just signed. He agreed with me that we might just be in for a difficult ride with our new Belgian signing. I wasn't looking forward at all to working with this surly character, however long he remained at Newcastle United.

My first impression of Philippe Albert was undoubtedly dreadful – and it turned out to be entirely wrong. Philippe was an absolute gentleman. He became one of the friendliest and most likeable footballers I ever had the pleasure of working with. Later that same year, I rehabilitated him from a career-threatening cruciate ligament injury. He was the model patient and working with him was a complete joy. He wasn't such a grumpy Belgian after all. In fact, he was rather charming. First impressions can be very deceiving.

A waste of time...

Manchester City came to St James' Park for a Coca-Cola Cup replay in December 1994. Newcastle United were flying high under Kevin Keegan and we were expected to win. I reported for work as usual about three hours before the fixture. I was busy making preparations for the Newcastle United players to arrive, when some suits adorned with the Manchester City crest appeared at our treatment room door. City's physiotherapist had been taken ill with a suspected hernia and like most teams in those days Manchester City travelled with only one physio. After a brief conversation with manager Kevin Keegan, it was agreed that I would be their physio for the night.

It was a very unnerving experience walking across the hall, entering the away changing room, and introducing myself to the bunch of strangers I hoped would be going home very disappointed at the end of the match. I needn't have worried. I was greeted enthusiastically by Brian Horton, the grateful manager, who took time to introduce me to each and every one of his players. They were as equally warm and friendly as their manager. Professional footballers and football changing rooms are the same all over the world. They are basically rooms filled with very talented working-class boys made good. The conversations are the same, the haircuts are the same, the music is the same. That was the case in 1994, and it will still be the case today. More importantly for me, that night the ankles, knees and backs were the same. It was easy for me to settle straight in and get on with preparing the players for what I hoped would be their inevitable defeat against my friends in the home dressing room.

The game didn't go the way we had anticipated. After 11 minutes and against all odds, Man City went 1-0 up through an Uwe Rösler goal at the Gallowgate end. Newcastle missed several chances to pull level before Paul Walsh put the visitors two up in the 80th minute. The stadium fell silent with the anticipation of another premature cup exit for Newcastle United. The only noise in the stunned stadium was emanating from the pocket of Man City supporters who were singing and dancing their way towards an unlikely victory on a cold December night. But they weren't there quite yet. Newcastle United was pushing hard for a goal that would bring us right back into the game and make for a nervy final 10 minutes for Man City.

I could feel the frustration, rippling from the stands, oozing from the home dugout and welling up inside me. We were desperate for something, anything to get us back into the game. The clock was ticking down fast. Every second mattered. Time was running out. Newcastle United was going out of the Coca-Cola Cup. We needed a miracle. I felt that sickening feeling we all get watching our team on the brink of defeat. It is that dull dread mixed with hope still that all football fans feel until the whistle blows and finally puts us out of our misery. The Newcastle players were piling forward in the only way Kevin Keegan's team knew how to play. The home team was attacking the Gallowgate End in wave after wave of attack. The pressure on the exhausted City players was intense. It felt like something had to give. Newcastle was going to score. Newcastle *must* score. It was relentless. Then, in the dying minutes, a City player suddenly crumpled in a heap, crying out in pain. He was in considerable distress. The game stopped. The momentum for the home team was lost. I raced onto St James' Park to treat the stricken player. I could hear his loud moans long before I reached the place where he was lying in obvious pain. The game no longer mattered. My only concern was for my distressed patient. I crouched down and put my bag on the pitch beside him. I tried to ascertain the cause of his agony.

'What's the problem?'

He instantly stopped groaning and smiled warmly.

'Absolutely nothing. No problem at all. Just stay with me for a minute.'

I looked into his face. He had a grin from ear to ear. I couldn't help but laugh with him and at the situation I found myself in.

'You do know I'm Newcastle's physio, don't you?'

I got up to leave. He held on to my arm. He wouldn't let go.

'I do know that, yes. Now, can I please have a drink of water?' There was nothing else I could do but give him his water. I stood there in the middle of St James' Park and helped him to run down the clock.

The Man City dressing room that night was exactly how you'd expect the away dressing room to be after a well-deserved victory against, what was on paper, a much stronger home team. It was a surreal place for me to be when I was employed by the club that had just been knocked out. I had a job to do, though, so I stayed in their victorious dressing room. I patched up their bumps and bruises while they celebrated their unexpected win against high-flying Newcastle United. I shook hands with many of them as they made their way to their coach. I returned to the eerily empty home dressing room and shared a beer with my deflated colleague Derek Wright.

I was glad to see the back of Manchester City and thought I would never hear from them again. I received a letter in the post a week or two later. It was a handwritten note from Brian Horton, the manager. He thanked me for my professionalism. A lovely and unnecessary gesture.

Gazza and a missing passport

The mid '90s was an incredible time to be a part of Newcastle United. The Kevin Keegan era was at its zenith, and in the 1995/96 season it looked and felt for a long time that the club would go on to lift the Premiership trophy. The improvements on the field of play were brilliantly obvious for all to admire. Additions like David Ginola, Les Ferdinand and Keith Gillespie to an already overachieving and exciting squad earned Newcastle United its well-deserved label: The Entertainers.

It wasn't just on the pitch that the club was evolving and striving for improvement. The stadium was extended and refurbished. The already enormous and passionate fanbase had swelled to record numbers. There was a buzz around the city again. Newcastle United was now a force to be reckoned with, at least on the surface. Behind the scenes, the club had a lot of catching up to do to be considered a leading player in the Premier League. The training facilities that greeted players like Ginola and Ferdinand were frankly not worthy of an average Second Division team, never mind a team challenging for the Premier League title. Maiden Castle in Durham was a vast improvement on the old Benwell site, but it was a facility owned by Durham University and designed to meet the needs of its students. The pitches were excellent, but everything else was average. The players shared their changing rooms with the students. The weights gym was a tiny room with an old multigym unit in the middle, and again this was shared with and often fully occupied by the students. The surface of the indoor playing area was a rock-hard health hazard to the club's prized assets. The medical room was two offices combined. In the upstairs canteen the only food on offer was a cup of soup. This was hardly the stuff of champions. If the club wanted to build on its success and attract world-class players, it needed big improvements.

Sir John Hall and his board of directors were acutely aware of the problem. That's why in many ways the club was such an exciting place to be in the mid '90s. Any suggestions we made as a medical and coaching staff were not only listened to, they were also enacted. One of our suggestions was to put in a state-of-the-art gym and treatment room at St James' Park before then moving it to a brand-new training facility. We weren't permitted to have a gym installed at Maiden Castle, so the stadium was the next best option.

The board agreed in principle to the gym at St James' Park and to move to a new training facility. There was only one caveat: if we were going to invest heavily in a gym, medical facilities and a new training ground, we should do so only after having explored other top-quality facilities, not just in this county but in Europe. At that time Italian clubs were considered the gold standard for such facilities. In February 1995, therefore, I was part of a four-man delegation from Newcastle United which visited Italy. We were there to assess the medical and coaching facilities of three Italian teams – Juventus, Roma and Lazio. It was a brilliant trip. I felt I was part of an organisation that was striving for greatness.

I was excited to visit all three famous clubs, but particularly keen to arrive at Lazio's training ground on the outskirts of Rome. An old friend and teammate of mine was on the playing staff. I hadn't seen him for eight years. In that time, our lives had taken us to very different places. Mine had taken me to the despair of losing my career, the death of my mother, homelessness and a seven-year fight to claw my way back into the industry that had left me on the scrapheap. My old teammate, Paul Gascoigne, had gone on to achieve superstardom and riches beyond his wildest dreams. I hoped I might meet with him in Rome. I wondered how much the fame and riches might have changed him. I was curious to find out if he remained the warm, funny, mischievous character I'd first played alongside on a cold night in Whitley Bay when he was 14 and I was 16.

When we arrived at Lazio's training facility, the team was already being put through its paces behind an enormous wire fence. I didn't hold out much hope that I'd see Gazza after all. We were getting ready to leave when a lone figure broke off from the rest of the group and came sprinting towards our delegation. Gazza opened the gate and greeted me with an excited hug and a familiar beaming grin. It was lovely to see him. We chatted like we were kids again. Nothing about him was any different to the friendly boy I remembered. He shouted towards the crowd seated in a small stand behind us. Out of that crowd trudged his boyhood friend Jimmy 'Five Bellies' Gardner. I knew Jimmy from my time with Paul at Newcastle. The disgruntled coach called for Gazza to rejoin the training session. He hugged me. He had rapid-fire instructions for Jimmy as he was leaving.

'Take Ferra [my nickname] and show him where the prostitutes are.'

I thanked him but declined the offer. With that, Gazza was gone. Jimmy remained. I couldn't help but notice he had a huge bump on his head. I asked him how he got it.

'Oh, that? Gazza telt me to get on the bonnet of his car and hang on. He was deeing donuts but then he stopped too quickly. I flew off and banged me fuckin' heed on the waal.'

I was still digesting the madness he was imparting when Jimmy began pleading with me. 'Can yee please ask Paul to give us me passport back?'

I asked him why Gazza was in possession of his passport.

'Well, you see, I usually fly back with him when he's home, 'cos he doesn't like flying on his own. Then I fly straight back to Newcastle. This time he kept me fuckin' passport, so I cannot gan home. I've only got this fuckin' shell suit I'm wearing and it's starting to stink an aal that.'

I asked him how long he'd been without his passport and wearing the same shell suit.

'It's been nearly three fuckin' weeks, man. Me missus is gan mad.'

Mad indeed! I didn't get the chance to ask Gazza to return Jimmy's passport. I presume he got it back eventually! Fame and fortune certainly hadn't changed Paul Gascoigne. I was proud of how far Gazza had come and of how little he had changed from the likable boy I'd once known.

Substance behind the style

The summer of 1995 was a seismic moment in Kevin Keegan's tenure as manager of Newcastle United. His remarkable transformation of the team was already very evident, but progress had stalled. Promotion at the end of the 1992/93 had been followed by a third place finish in 1993/94. In January of the following season, prolific striker Andy Cole was sold. It was a move that stunned not only football but Andy, too. I can still recall him sitting in the treatment room at Maiden Castle, shaking his head in bewilderment that he was on his way to Manchester United. The brilliant Keith Gillespie moved the other way as part of the deal. At that time, the manager's masterstroke, in securing Keith as a makeweight in the deal, wasn't fully appreciated by many inside or outside the club.

Kevin had to deal very publicly with some unrest. His confrontation with fans on the steps of St James' Park was beamed around the world. The team finished in a very commendable sixth place that season, but Kevin made it abundantly clear in the dressing room on the final day, that this simply wasn't good enough. It would be embarrassing, he told the players, to walk around the pitch on the traditional end of season lap of honour, when both he and they had let the supporters down. He was a fiercely driven individual who demanded incredibly high standards from himself and all those who were under his command. That fact was never more apparent to me than when listening to him that day. I was fascinated to see what he would do next.

Signing Les Ferdinand, David Ginola, Warren Barton and Shaka Hislop, that summer of 1995, was what he did next.

They were brilliant additions and all contributed to what would become one of the great teams in modern Newcastle United history. Of the four marquee signings, it was perhaps David Ginola who raised the most eyebrows. A quick glance at his career statistics indicated he was a very successful, international performer, but he was relatively unknown in this country. I'd never heard of him until the press began suggesting he might be on his way to Celtic or Newcastle United.

Like many others, I didn't really know what to expect. On his first day in training, he came into the treatment room looking more like a Hollywood actor than a footballer. Tall, impossibly handsome, all teeth, tan and hair. Full of Gallic charm and bonhomie. That afternoon I was chatting with Steve Howey, who gave me an early indication of what kind of signing we'd made. After I asked how David had performed in training, he laughed.

'He was unbelievable. His first touch is brilliant, he can turn either way, use either foot, can take a tackle, and he's as strong as an ox. If he does that on a match day, fuck me, what a player we have!'

Steve's description ensured I couldn't wait to see how David performed. When I did watch him in those first few months, I couldn't really believe what I was seeing. Forget the glamour, the Hollywood good looks, the tan and teeth, David Ginola was a world-class footballer and one of the best I have ever had the pleasure of seeing play in a Newcastle United shirt. He became more famous for his looks and style than he did for his footballing ability – but there was much more to David than style. David Ginola was a man of enormous strength and character. As a footballer there was an abundance of substance behind the style.

The versatility and timekeeping of Faustino Asprilla

Tino Asprilla arrived in February 1996 in a snowstorm. The mercurial Columbian came with a somewhat wayward reputation. I wasn't sure what to expect. He was already a superstar who had set the football world alight in Italy, both on and off the field. He arrived with an entourage that included his own medical guru.

Medical gurus often set alarm bells ringing in my head. Over the years I have met many. The vast majority had absolutely no formal qualifications in medicine or any other associated profession. They tended to be someone who'd befriended a famous player, who would then recommend their services to other impressionable individuals only too happy to part with their cash in exchange for some questionable dietary advice, exercise protocol or other general bullshittery.

As it happened, Tino's medical guru was a qualified doctor. He was a lovely, unassuming man who was a very helpful asset when it came to managing some of the issues Tino had with his overall fitness and wellbeing. Tino would go on to spend nearly two unforgettable years on Tyneside. He was an absolute joy to be around, a wonderfully eccentric character who fully embraced his time at the club. His skills on the pitch were like nothing any of us had seen before. His long elastic legs seemed to move in a way others simply couldn't. Sometimes, his control of the football was mesmerising. At other times he looked like he'd never played the game before. When he was bad, he was really bad, but when he was good, he was brilliant.

I can still visualise him bamboozling the defender with his movement, leaping off the ground, gliding majestically through the air before his head made beautiful contact with Keith Gillespie's perfect cross to score the third goal of his unforgettable hat-trick against the mighty Barcelona at St James' Park. It was one of the most exhilarating sights I have ever seen on a football pitch. Tino spent the hour before that game in the bowels of the stadium, with his gangly legs hanging over his guru's shoulders as his Columbian doctor bent, stretched and twisted his patient's body in ways I had never seen before and have never seen since. I hated gurus, but I made an exception for Tino's. Whatever he was doing, worked.

It wasn't just on the pitch that Tino made a splash. He was prolific in the nightclubs of the city as well. There wasn't a week would pass without some incident or other that the football club had to manage. He was like a box of fireworks, both on and off the pitch. I was sorry to see him go when he departed, all too soon.

Several years later, I was having dinner with Kevin Keegan, who told me my favourite ever tale of the many involving Tino and his time at Newcastle United. Tino had arrived in the snow accompanied by his agent. Neither of them spoke very much English, if any at all. Kevin set them down. He wanted to address Tino's reputation.

'I'm thinking about playing Tino this afternoon.'

There were blank expressions and no responses from Tino or his agent. Kevin tried again.

'Tino's a great player, but I am a little bit concerned about his temperament.'

Again there was no response from Tino or his agent. Kevin began to get a little exasperated. He made one final effort to address his concerns around Tino's temperament.

'He's very volatile.'

There was once again no response from Tino. There was, however, finally a flicker behind the eyes of the agent. He sighed, grateful that he'd finally understood what Kevin was trying to convey. He nodded in agreement and responded enthusiastically.

'Ah, yes... he velly volatile! He can play right. He can play left. He can play down the middle. He velly velly volatile!'

Kevin smiled, nodded and gave up.

One of Tino Asprilla's more annoying traits was his inability to be on time for training, meetings or matches. He was late for training every day of his time at the club, apart from one notable exception. I arrived at the training ground on a Sunday morning in late October 1996, and flicked on the treatment room lights to find Tino fast asleep. I shook him from his slumber. He rubbed his eyes and spoke to me in broken English. He pointed to his expensive watch. He wanted to know where everyone else was. I still to this day don't think he fully understood what I was trying to tell him about the clocks having gone back an hour the night before.

Tino Asprilla was certainly a one-off. An unpredictable but brilliant one-off.

The smiling assassin

I met Les Ferdinand by chance in the summer of 2024. We bumped into each other in the reception of a hotel in his home city of London. He greeted me with a beaming smile. It was the exact same smile I had seen every day for the two seasons he spent at Newcastle United. Few players have left such an impression on the club having spent such a relatively short time in the north-east. He arrived with a reputation for being a little injury-prone. We were nervous about that in the treatment room. We shouldn't have been. The only time I saw him in there was because he made a point of coming in every day to have a laugh and a joke. He was the most laid-back and affable of characters off the pitch. On it, he could leap like a salmon, run like a gazelle, and score goals. His goals nearly took Newcastle United all the way to the title in his first season – and won him the PFA Player of the Year. The following season he teamed up with Alan Shearer to form the most lethal of partnerships. If there was any apprehension around how these two superstar centre-forwards and big personalities would gel, there really shouldn't have been. Off the pitch they got on like a house on fire. On the pitch they set the house on fire. Together, they terrorised defences during the 1996/97 season. Alan Shearer was as phenomenal as we all hoped he would be. Les Ferdinand played his brilliantly destructive part with a permanent smile on his face. The smiling assassin.

The Fulwell End is always full…

Alan Shearer joined his boyhood club in the summer of 1996 as the world's most expensive footballer. A Geordie boy coming home in triumph. I had the great honour of playing a small part in his medical on the day he signed for the club. I travelled with the club secretary, Russell Cushing, to meet with Alan and his agent Tony Stephens at a private hospital in Manchester. We were driven to what was supposedly a top-secret meeting in a Bentley bearing NUFC number plates. Unsurprisingly, it didn't take long for the press to find us.

To be part of what was then a world record transfer was an exhilarating experience. Alan Shearer's goals at Euro 96 had brought England tantalisingly close to lifting its first trophy since 1966. It didn't matter what part of the country you were from, either: the team's performances had electrified the nation. For most of the summer, Alan looked like he would be leaving Blackburn Rovers and heading to the recently crowned Premier League champions, Manchester United. So when I got a call from Russell Cushing to tell me I was on my way to Manchester to perform part of the medical for a new player we were signing that day, I didn't for a moment believe we would be signing Alan Shearer for a world-record fee.

Russell had refused to tell me the name of the player I would be meeting later that day. So when I opened the door of the treatment room and saw the great man lying on the couch, I felt my heart thump. I took a sharp intake of breath to compose myself. Then I casually strolled over and shook his hand. I carried out my examinations as if I examined world-record superstar footballers on a regular basis. I got very acquainted with Alan very soon when I had to insert my finger up his scrotum to assess his recently repaired hernia. I find that a finger up the scrotum is a good ice-breaker in any situation.

When the examination was complete, my famous patient joined me for tea and biscuits. We chatted for an hour or two while Tony and Russell completed formalities. By the end of that conversation,

I was no longer chatting to a world-famous footballer, I was chatting to someone I instinctively liked and who I was certain would become a friend. Alan remains that to this day. He has been a supporter of mine in good times, a confidant in difficult times, and a rock in hard times. That day, I realised Newcastle United were getting a special character as well as a special player. I also knew that Alan Shearer's passion for his boyhood club burned ferociously. He talked of two things during our conversation: his family and Newcastle United. He was a fan, a fanatic, and now the team's centre-forward. He was about to live his dream and couldn't wait to get started.

A few weeks later, on 4 September, we travelled to Sunderland for the Tyne–Wear derby game. Most of the squad were still getting to know the character of the new superstar in our midst. The atmosphere outside and inside the stadium was feral. We were greeted by a sea of red and white vitriol. No away fans were allowed into the ground. There would be no chanting Newcastle fans to counteract the fierce noise that would undoubtedly erupt from the Fulwell End, where the diehard Sunderland fans congregated for every game.

In the changing room before the game, it was quiet and tense. Too tense. You could feel the collective nervousness and apprehension in the room. Then, from somewhere in the corner, someone started to sing. It wasn't a song that the other players knew. I recognised it immediately. It was a song I'd heard sung at St James' Park from back when I had been a player. Tonight, the song boomed from one voice and filled the room like a lion's roar. The world's most expensive footballer stood up and, to the tune of 'When the Saints Go Marching In', belted out this very colourful terrace song from his days as a boy supporting Newcastle United:

The Fulwell End (the Fulwell End)
Is always full (is always full)
The Fulwell End is always full (full of what?)
Full of shit, full of piss, full of wankers,
The Fulwell End is always full

That diffused the tension in the dressing room. Cheers and laughter from his new teammates completely changed the atmosphere. The other players recognised that the world superstar was also simply a boy from the terraces of St James' Park. We won the game. That wasn't the last time we heard Alan Shearer sing at a Tyne–Wear Derby.

The Sunderland fans have many colourful chants of their own. One such chant was directed at our Sunderland-born centre-half, Steve Howey. Steve came through the youth system and was a fantastic player for Newcastle United during the Kevin Keegan era. His brother, Lee, played for Sunderland. Both teams were in the tunnel at St James' Park. It is always an incredibly tense moment and a charged atmosphere. Old enemies standing cheek to jowl in the tight space before they enter the cauldron of heat and noise where they will do fierce battle. For Steve playing for Newcastle, and for Lee playing for Sunderland, the tension must have been especially stifling. Not this night, it wasn't. The eerie silence in the tunnel was broken abruptly when Alan Shearer burst into terrace chanting once more. This time, he did so at the expense of Steve Howey, his teammate, and to the delight of everyone else in the narrow space. Both teams took to the pitch still laughing at what they'd just heard. Alan Shearer, the Newcastle United captain, singing a less than complimentary song about his own teammate. With his tongue firmly in his cheek, Alan sang for the amusement of both teams.

'Lee Howey, Lee Howey, Lee Howey
Your brother is a cunt!'

It was a favourite chant of the Sunderland fans. There have been better Sunderland terrace chants created. I bet that none of the others have ever been sung in the tunnel of St James' Park by the Newcastle United captain, though.

Shear brilliance

It's difficult to convey the level of hysteria that swept the northeast when Alan Shearer opted to join his hometown club instead of heading to the recently crowned champions, Manchester United. In his previous three seasons at Blackburn, Alan had proven himself to be the best centre-forward of his generation. His goals had almost single-handedly won England its first major tournament in 30 years at Euro 96. Newcastle United had very nearly won the title in 1996. With Alan Shearer coming home, silverware felt guaranteed. Sadly, the silverware eluded Alan and the club, but what we were treated to in Alan Shearer's record-breaking 10 years at Newcastle United will never be repeated. He plundered goals. He suffered not one, but two career-threatening injuries. He plundered more goals. On many occasions he carried the team on his broad shoulders. He plundered yet more goals. Who can forget the thud from his electric right boot before the abused ball ripped into the roof of the Everton net at the Gallowgate End? Or the deafening noise from the Gallowgate the day he broke Jackie Milburn's Newcastle United goalscoring record against Portsmouth? The roar that day surpassed even the moment when Kevin Keegan scored on his debut back in May 1982.

Alan Shearer ended his stellar career as the Premier League's all-time leading goal scorer with 260 goals. He scored a record total of 206 goals in all competitions for Newcastle United. Not bad for a man who suffered a total of three career-threatening injuries (one at Blackburn, two at Newcastle). He was a world-beater in black and white. A bona fide local hero.

When he announced his retirement in 2006, he said, 'When I was a boy, I wanted to wear the number nine shirt and score goals at St James' Park. I've lived my dream.'

You wore it well, Alan. We all lived the dream.

An unhappy manager, a Christmas do and a pink tutu

Nowadays, the footballers' Christmas party usually involves a trip on a private jet to a party city in the UK or perhaps sometimes even a jaunt to an exotic location abroad. The vast wealth of the players these days means that nowhere and nothing is off the table. When I was a young player in the 1980s, no Christmas do was complete without drinking ourselves into oblivion. Then after falling over, or vomiting, or often both, we'd all file into the backroom of some dingy pub, where it was compulsory to laugh at the very blue jokes of the decidedly average comedian. After he left the stage, the customary strippers would replace him to raucous applause and shockingly inappropriate comments. Invariably one of the younger members of the squad would be press-ganged into becoming part of the performance.

The Christmas 'do' in whatever its form has always been a big deal for footballers. The 1990s were no exception. If anything, I think the '90s were the high point for the footballers' Christmas party. It was the biggest event in the social calendar by far. To be elected as the organiser was a great honour for any player. Preparations often began in early August. Why was, and is it, such a big deal? Simply, I think, because the football season is a long one. Players and staff sacrifice the Christmas festivities with their families so that fans can watch the traditional Christmas fixtures. The 'do' takes on a life of its own. Lots of thought and planning is involved and everyone looks forward to it.

Newcastle United's Christmas do in 1996 was to be a fancy dress party. They were all the rage back then. Weeks of discussions on potential outfit choices were followed by hours of traipsing around the various fancy dress outfitters in the north-east. I chose my outfit during a visit to one of the shops in Newcastle city centre. My friend, and fellow physiotherapist, Derek Wright accompanied me. To my surprise, he bounded straight to the counter and asked the young girl there if she had a particular outfit he had in mind. When I heard what he had in mind, I did wonder what was going on in his head. I left the shop happy with my choice. Rather worryingly, so did Derek.

We counted down the days and we were both looking forward to letting our hair down and donning our outfits. Unfortunately, the day before the party a complaint was made to Kevin Keegan about the behaviour of two of our senior players during a recent hotel stay. It was a relatively minor incident. Some high jinks in the reception area had damaged a chair leg. It was a trivial incident at best, but Kevin Keegan didn't see it like that. In Kevin's eyes, any breach of discipline was sullying the good name of Newcastle United. Derek had also been at the hotel, and received phone calls from both players involved to say that they'd been on the end of a ticking-off from their ultra-professional manager.

On the morning of the party, Derek was a nervous wreck. He spent his time watching the treatment room door for the moment Kevin Keegan would inevitably pop his head through and summon him to his office next door. I tried to reassure my friend. I knew how much Kevin genuinely liked and respected Derek Wright. We all did. Whatever was to come, was very unlikely to change Kevin's opinion.

Kevin made him stew all morning. Derek started to relax and believe he was actually going to escape the manager's wrath after all. Then, just as we were about to get changed into our fancy dress outfits, Kevin's familiar features filled the doorway to our treatment room. Derek followed his boss into the office next door. Steve Howey, one of the player's involved, stood waiting for them dressed from head to toe as an emu. Kevin gave his star centre-half a double take and a stern head shake. I don't think the emu outfit helped Kevin's mood. It certainly didn't help the mild-mannered Derek Wright. That afternoon of the do the Newcastle United manager gave Derek Wright the dressing-down of his life. It was as brutal as it was harsh. I could hear Kevin shouting and swearing from his office next to the treatment room.

'I've lost all respect for you, Derek. You're supposed to be a fucking professional. You're not here to be the players' fucking mate. You're not here to be a figure of fucking fun. I will never look at you the same way again . . .'

Derek Wright was crestfallen when he came back to the treatment room. Tearful. I reminded him that we were already late and we needed to don our fancy dress outfits for the team photo that was to take place outside Kevin's office. He shook his head.

'I just can't, Paul. I can't put that outfit on. I can't go to the party. Not after that.'

I felt very sorry for him. I was also selfishly looking forward to the party. I knew that if my friend and physio colleague didn't go, then it would be entirely wrong for me to go without him. I really wanted to go! I talked Derek around for 20 minutes. I told him the do wasn't about what Kevin had said; rather, it was a reward for all of his hard work throughout the year. I had some convincing to do.

'Yes, the telling-off was brutal. Yes, the manager is angry with you. But Kevin respects you. Kevin knows deep down that you're a brilliant professional. More importantly he knows you're an honest man. A good man. Don't let the timing of a stupid telling-off that will be probably forgotten tomorrow, spoil a day you've been looking forward to for months. Surely you can see that this is just a timing issue. If the rollocking had happened last week you wouldn't think twice about going to the party. I guarantee you Kevin will have forgotten all about the matter in a couple of days. If you don't go to the party, all you'll have done is allow bad timing to ruin the biggest night of the year for you.'

It's amazing how persuasive I can be when I want to go to a party! Derek took comfort from my words and heeded my advice. He rushed off to get changed, and was ready before me. He strolled outside to where the players were congregated. I put on my hippy beard and moustache and made my way past Kevin's office. Suddenly, there was an eruption of laughter coming from outside Kevin's window. The curious manager climbed onto a chair and opened the narrow slot to establish the source of the merriment. He shook his head and turned to climb down from his chair. He caught sight of me as I slipped past his door.

'You! Come here! Come and see your mate.'

He climbed back up on the chair. His hippy physiotherapist climbed up beside him. Kevin poked his disgusted finger out of the window, while I lowered my John Lennon shades and followed his outstretched and outraged arm. I had to stifle a laugh as I watched the entire playing staff of Newcastle United rolling on the floor with their legs in the air like they were the Martians from the old Smash adverts. They were howling. Howling as their much-loved and well-respected physiotherapist Derek Wright plodded proudly towards them. He was wearing an ill-fitting pink tutu that didn't fasten properly over his ample backside, accompanied by a two-foot high Marie Antionette wig. A pair of DM's, a sparkling fairy wand and a full face of powder and make-up completed his outfit. It was a sight to behold for the players and certainly merited the laughter it drew.

It was something else entirely for Kevin Keegan and me as we stared at Derek's exposed rear end. I pushed my sunglasses up over my eyes, hoping that by doing so, I could slip off the chair without our apoplectic manager noticing. Kevin was still shaking his head as he grabbed my flowery kaftan.

'What have I just said to him about not being a figure of fun? I'm wasting my bloody time!'

I nodded in meek agreement. There wasn't much else I could do when I was standing in front of him dressed as a hippy who wouldn't have been out of place at Woodstock.

It won Derek first prize for the best fancy dress costume of the night. It was one hell of an outfit. It did him no harm with Kevin either. The manager continued to respect Derek who was a most loyal and dedicated servant of Newcastle United.

I do sometimes wonder still as to what must go on inside the mind of a man who walks into a fancy dress outfitters and specifically asks for a pink tutu and a Marie Antionette wig. Then determines that the outfit won't be fully complete without a fairy wand and DM's! Derek has never explained his thinking to me – or to anyone else for that matter.

The pride of Cookstown

When I made my debut for Newcastle United on 1 May, 1982, I was acutely aware that I was the first boy from Northern Ireland to do so since the great David Craig, back in 1963. The path from Northern Ireland, through the youth set-up and into the first team, wasn't well-trodden. So, when a young boy from Northern Ireland signed as an apprentice at the club in 1995, I was particularly interested in how he would progress, especially as he played for Lisburn Youth, my former boys club. I was also acutely aware of just how lonely a place the world can seem after you've left behind family and friends in Ireland for a new life in England when you are little more than a child.

It was with that thought in mind that my wife Geraldine and I invited 16-year-old Aaron Hughes to the Metrocentre, soon after he signed in 1995. The purpose of the lunch was to establish how he was finding the change and to let him know that we were always around if ever he needed to chat, away from the club, to people from back home who'd once made the same journey. I left that first meeting with Aaron worried about his chances of making it as a footballer. I knew nothing of his ability, but the boy who sat in front of us that day was incredibly shy, impeccably polite and impossibly nervous. He was so polite he wouldn't even allow us to buy him a sandwich, or indeed spend any money on him that day. He was a gentleman no doubt, but was he too gentle to cope with the rough and tumble of a professional football career? I hoped not, but I feared the worst. But then, what the hell do I know!

Aaron Hughes made his debut at the Nou Camp two years later and established himself as a regular under Sir Bobby Robson. He made nearly 200 appearances for the club. He played all along the back four and occasionally in midfield. I don't remember him having a bad game. He left in 2005. In his impressive football career, Aaron made over 500 senior appearances for several clubs. Added to that, he represented Northern Ireland, with distinction, 112 times. He did all of that while remaining the quiet, polite, impeccable gentleman who wouldn't let me buy him a sandwich in 1995.

Aaron Hughes was one of the most impressive individuals I met in my entire time in professional football. He is the pride of his hometown of Cookstown, the best thing to come out of there since the sausages (if you know, you know!).

An enthusiastic student

I was always wary of having physiotherapy students come into the club. I just felt that even if someone wanted to work as a physio in professional football they'd first have to go through the university and hospital systems. For that reason, it seemed to me more logical for students to shadow a physiotherapist in a clinical setting in a hospital. I had one absolute red line: I wouldn't accept any request from individuals who were not already enrolled on a physiotherapy degree course. That may seem a pretty uncharitable approach. After all, what better way for someone to get a foot on the ladder into the privileged world of professional football than spending time at a club, getting to know the players and staff, and, more importantly, displaying a spectacular personality, good manners and all-round suitability for future employment in that usually closed-off world? It may well have been uncharitable of me to deny others the opportunity to find a pathway into professional football, but I was comfortable with my approach.

I hadn't always been so strict. I used to welcome all comers into the treatment room. I would play host to physio students, medical students, sports science students and any girl or boy of any age who expressed even the slightest bit of interest in wanting to pursue a career in physiotherapy within professional football. There came a point when I changed my mind, and after that breaking into Fort Knox was easier than getting a placement within the physiotherapy department at Newcastle United. I refused all requests – unless the applicant was a final-year physiotherapy student. Then they were more than welcome to spend three weeks in our department.

It was a restrictive rule, but I still quite regularly had students shadow me during my 13 years as a physio at the club. That did sometimes present challenges. Some students were more capable than others; some were more memorable than others; and some were evidently there simply so they could get closer to their heroes. Of all the students I welcomed, one lives longer in my memory than all of the others combined. He was quite simply the most inquisitive, dedicated and incredibly intense student I ever worked with. From the moment he walked through the door, he followed me everywhere, except to the bathroom. He scrutinised every move I made and dissected every conversation I had with my patients. I would be having a quiet word with our star striker when I'd feel my student's breath on my neck and his eyes boring through my head. I'd sit down for a well-earned break at the end of the day and he'd sidle up and interrogate me for the next hour or two on my rationale for recommending a particular treatment protocol, why I examined a knee in a certain way, or why I'd chosen a particular tone to speak to one player yet adopted an entirely different one for another player. All the while, he'd be furiously scribbling my replies into his notepad. It was very intense. His thirst for learning was unquenchable. In the end, he drove me to absolute distraction!

One memorable day, he outdid himself for intensity and misplaced enthusiasm. I was called out of the treatment room to tend to someone who'd injured himself badly while playing five-a-side in the main gym. We trained at Durham University's recreational facility, sharing the premises with student lecturers and members of the public. I ran as quickly as I could to establish what the fuss was about. My student ran with me. There was a huge throng of students and lecturers crowding around a thirty-something man lying screaming on the floor. I looked at his lower leg and the source of his pain was blindingly obvious: a compound fracture of his tibia and fibula. The bones were shattered and poking out through his skin. His lower leg was bent from the fracture site, as if he had two knee joints. It was the worst fracture I'd ever seen. No wonder the poor man was still screaming so loudly as I crouched down beside him.

My student knelt down opposite me, pen and paper at the ready, eager to capture my words of wisdom to the stricken stranger who now lay shaking with shock. I leaned across the patient and quietly informed my student that the patient had a compound fracture. I then calmly informed him that that we needed an ambulance as quickly as possible. I spent the rest of the time reassuring our patient that all was in hand and that all would be well. I got him painkillers, and some pillows to support his head and fracture site. I covered him in a blanket and asked the curious onlookers to leave him in peace. I basically just kept him as calm and comfortable as possible until the paramedics arrived and took him to the local hospital so that he could receive the emergency care he so obviously needed. There was nothing I or anyone else could do for him. I'm glad to say the ambulance was with us in a matter of minutes and the crisis was over almost as quickly as it had begun.

That afternoon I was getting showered. I opened my cubicle door, only to be met by my student and his notepad. As I covered my modesty, he was already in full interrogation mode. He wanted to know every minute detail of what I'd done and why I'd done it.

'It was so impressive how you dealt with everything. I don't think I'll ever be able to do what you did. I mean your differential diagnosis of a compound fracture was amazing. How did you reach that diagnosis so quickly? It was fantastic.'

His pen was at the ready for me to give him the rundown on my brilliance as a physiotherapist. He stared intently into my face. That was the final straw. He never asked me another question after the response I gave him that day. I'm not proud of my reply. I stood naked with my arms outstretched.

'For fuck's sake, man. His bones were sticking out of his fucking leg! There was no differential diagnosis. You don't even need to be a fucking physio to diagnose that. You just need to look with your fucking eyes, man!'

That was the last interaction I ever had with him. My student shadowed Derek Wright for the rest of his time with us. Derek was a very patient man, but even he was very relieved when our overly enthusiastic student and his ever-present notepad left the building for the final time. I'm not sure whether or not our student ever pursued a career in physiotherapy. I suspect he might have become an investigative journalist instead. He was certainly more suited.

A Yorkshire terrier

When Newcastle United signed David Batty in 1996, the club was acquiring the services of a born winner. David had won the old Football League First Division title with Leeds United and the Premier League with Blackburn Rovers. He was widely regarded as one of the best defensive midfielders in the country. Over the years we'd all seen him snapping and snarling his way through games, sometimes even fighting his own teammates. There appeared to be little creativity to his game. In many ways, he was portrayed as a somewhat unsavoury character. How wrong both stereotypes were! The quietly spoken man, who introduced himself to me on his first day at the club, was very different to the one I'd anticipated meeting. On the pitch, too, there was so much more to David Batty's game than I'd ever imagined. I loved watching him play. He was a fiercely competitive and supremely intelligent footballer. Off the pitch, he proved to be an enormously likeable family man, and I was sorry to see him leave in 1998.

David Batty – a proud Yorkshire man, more gentleman than terrier.

A Psycho mummy

It was brilliantly refreshing when a player arrived with a big reputation and an incredible career behind him, then turned out to be humble, grounded and likeable. There were quite a few who fell into that category – Alan Shearer, Gary Speed, David Batty and John Barnes spring instantly to mind. And then there was Stuart Pearce. 'Psycho', as he was nicknamed by his adoring fans at Nottingham Forest, played for Newcastle towards the end of his outstanding career. He formed an instant bond with my physio colleague Derek Wright, mainly over their shared love of punk music. He stayed in Derek's house for a lot of the time he was with the club. He was down to earth and honest, and shunned the typical footballer lifestyle. Years of plying his trade on the non-league circuit with Wealdstone, while working as an electrician, ensured Stuart was one of the most grounded professional footballers I ever met. He was a scarily fierce competitor

Stuart Pearce strikes a pose. A great footballer. A very humble man. A fine gentleman.

on the field and a complete gentleman off it. From the moment I met him on the day he signed until the day he left, I thoroughly enjoyed his company. I loved his professionalism and really liked his down-to-earth personality. He was a complete one-off. A throwback to a time before the game had drowned in money and the Sky TV cameras had turned too many average players into multimillionaire household names. Stuart Pearce struck me as someone who was only interested in being a great footballer and a good person. He succeeded spectacularly at both.

It was early December 1997. The morning of the fancy dress Christmas party. Stuart was in his usual place, sitting at our small desk in the corner of our treatment room. He spent every morning there debating the latest issues of the day with John Barnes, Derek and me. I asked Stuart what outfit he was planning to wear for the Christmas party that night.

'Outfit. What d'you mean outfit? I haven't got an outfit. I don't DO fancy dress bollocks.'

It was clear he had paid no attention to the preparations, the dress code, the date, or the possible sanctions he was facing for non-compliance. He shrugged his shoulders and intimated he would just turn up in his normal clothing. His punk spirit was very evident that morning. I gently reminded him of the consequences.

'You can't just turn up, I'm afraid. Unfortunately, an outfit is compulsory. Anyone who doesn't wear fancy dress is subject to a sizable fine. You –'

'Oh fuck off! A fucking fine for refusing to make a complete dick of myself?'

There was silence in the treatment room. Then Stuart got to his feet and began opening and shutting cupboard doors. He didn't find what he was looking for and slumped back down on his chair.

'What kind of treatment room doesn't even have any bandages?'

I walked to the door that led out to the narrow hallway which housed our store cupboard. I carried a box full of bandages back into the room and sat them on his lap.

'You only had to ask.'

He smiled, apologised for being a grumpy bastard and left the room with six or seven bandages and a roll of sticky tape.

The fancy dress party was held that evening in one of the lounges within the bowels of the Milburn Stand at St James' Park. All of the players and all of the staff were there. All of their wives and girlfriends, too. There were some memorable outfits on show. Clearly no expense had been spared. There were a lot of contenders for the best outfit of the night. Alan Shearer, Rob Lee and their wives were a very impressive ABBA. Steve Watson, Shaka Hislop and their wives were the swelteringly hot Teletubbies. The ever erratic and enigmatic Tino Asprilla came dressed as an extra from a spaghetti western, in a cowboy outfit accessorised with two ominously authentic-looking pistols. There were heavily made-up Disney princesses, a burly Spice Girls quintet and scores of other brilliant outfits – and howls of laughter and raucous cheers each time a new outfit or group entered the room.

There may well have been many contenders for best outfit but there was one clear winner. From the moment he appeared as a silhouette in the doorway before marching straight onto the empty dancefloor to take a well-deserved round of applause, Stuart Pearce, the man who that morning hadn't even possessed an outfit and had no intention of wearing one until he realised he'd have to pay a fine, raised his hands in celebration before bowing to his adoring public. I think at that moment I was the only person in the room that realised the man covered from head to toe in bandages and sporting a pair of dark shades was in fact the former England captain. It was genius. It hadn't cost him a penny, or a moment of preparation, but it was genius and one of the funniest sights I ever witnessed in all my time at the club. I told him how impressed I was.

'Your outfit is inspired, Brilliant. Very clever. Well done.'

Stuart shook his head. He wasn't having any of my praise.

'Not so fast. It ain't that fucking clever.'

I was undeterred.

'Don't be so modest, man. It's genius.'

He sat his beer down.

'I'll tell you how genius it is. I'm sweating my bollocks off in it and now I need a piss. I'll have to take the whole lot off and put it back on again after or I'm getting fined, aren't I? Fucking stupid bandages.'

With that, the sweaty mummy was on his feet and heading for the bathroom. The bandage around his left leg began to unravel as he made his way across the dance floor. He came back 15 minutes later minus the rest of his outfit. I handed him his beer. I reminded him he was getting fined. He was nonplussed.

'Fuck the fine. I'll pay double not to have to wear that shit.'

He didn't get fined in the end. He didn't deserve to be. Besides, I don't think anyone had the courage to ask the Psycho mummy for the money. I know I didn't.

Talking to Bruce Fucking Springsteen

In 1998, Stiff Little Fingers, the Irish punk band, played Newcastle Riverside. Although I wasn't the most avid fan, I loved their biggest hit, 'Alternative Ulster', from back in the heyday of punk. So, when Stuart Pearce asked my physio colleague Derek Wright and me to accompany him to the gig, I didn't hesitate. We warmed up for the gig with a few pints and a few laughs. The band took to the stage, and through my drunken haze – and to my great surprise – I noticed a very familiar face playing the bass guitar. Bruce Foxton from The Jam was a member of Stiff Little Fingers! I subsequently discovered he'd been an integral member for several years previously, too. I told you I wasn't a big fan!

The gig was brilliant. The alcohol helped. As the band left the stage to rapturous applause from middle aged punks, Stuart Pearce brought us backstage to meet his friend, the lead singer Jake Burns. We had several more beers with the band, and engaged in warm conversation with Bruce Foxton. It was a real honour to spend some time with someone who was a huge part of my adolescence. I can still remember a Sunday night in March 1980, anxiously waiting for the Radio 1 Top 40 countdown, hoping 'Going Underground' had made it to Number 1. As the DJ delivered his good news, my boyhood friend danced around our sitting room in his parka with *The Jam* emblazoned across his back.

In spite of working daily with world-famous footballers I was, in truth, more than a little starstruck by Bruce Foxton. He was a charming, unassuming character who gave us plenty of his time and regaled us with stories of his experiences in the music business. We talked for more than an hour over too many beers. He talked candidly about his career in The Jam, what he had done since the band broke up and of his life in general. I told him about my friend dancing around our sitting room. I also told him I was there when The Jam played its last ever televised gig on the first ever recording of *The Tube* in Newcastle in 1982. That was the point when I'm sure I saw Bruce Foxton's eyes glaze over. I politely asked him where I might find the bathroom. He was very happy to point me towards the door that led to a narrow corridor. I bounced off the walls on my way to the bathroom. Derek Wright bounced along behind me.

We were washing our hands at the sink. I looked at Derek through the dirty mirror with a crack running all the way through it. It distorted his face, but couldn't disguise his obvious excitement at how our night had panned out. I'd never seen him so animated. He stared back at me through the broken mirror. He threw his arm around my shoulder. He pulled me into his chest for a painful bear hug. He rubbed his knuckle through my hair. That was bloody sore too. The alcohol dulled the pain. He let me go. I fixed my hair and rubbed my sore neck.

'That hurt, you know,' I told the cracked mirror. I may as well have told the nicotine-stained wall. He paid no attention to my protestations. Instead he pulled me in again and rubbed his knuckle over my head.

'Ah, fuck off, man, you miserable bastard. What a night, eh? What a fucking night!'

He was oblivious to my sore head and strangled neck. Elated. Ecstatic. He was having the night of his life. He moved in for a third bear hug. I weaved out of his way. He needed to share his obvious excitement with the mirror and me.

'Fucking hell, son. Can you believe it, Paul? You and me, in there, talking to Bruce Fucking Springsteen! It's fucking unbelievable, son.'

I laughed.

'I think you mean Bruce Fucking Foxton, Derek.'

He splashed cold water on his face.

'What?'

'It's Bruce Foxton, not Bruce Springsteen, man!'

He splashed some more water on his face.

'Oh, fuck. So it is.'

On exiting the bathroom, the first person we bumped into was Bruce Foxton. I told him Derek thought he was Bruce Springsteen. We didn't stay long after that.

The General

The £700,000 paid to Charlton Athletic by Newcastle United for the services of Robert Lee in 1992 has to be some of the smartest money the club has ever spent. When the ever-persuasive Kevin Keegan convinced Londoner Rob that Second Division Newcastle was closer to London than First Division Middlesborough, even he can't have truly envisaged what a brilliant piece of business it would prove to be. Rob, a former wide player, blossomed into one of the great box to box midfielders of the newly formed Premier League. He was a dynamic link between an often beleaguered defence and the exhilarating front line. He had energy and could pass, dribble and tackle. He also had an eye for goal. He was outstanding under Kevin Keegan and Kenny Dalglish. He fell out of favour under Ruud Gullit, as many senior players did, and then had a brilliant renaissance as one of Sir Bobby Robson's blue chip boys. Robert Lee spent 10 years on Tyneside. He played over 300 games for the club. I can't remember him having a bad one. When the lists of all-time great Premier League midfielders are written, Robert Lee's name is often missing. It shouldn't be. He was that good.

A fan in the treatment room

By 1998, it was evident that we needed another member of staff for the physiotherapy department of Newcastle United. There were occasions during the previous season and this where it was proving very difficult to have a day off once a week. With the stunning success of the last few seasons came European games on top of an already busy schedule, and we in the medical department were struggling. I had a young family and was very conscious that, if the current work schedule was to continue, then most likely, I'd have to make a decision. Did I stay at the club and miss every family occasion, or leave professional football behind forever so that I could enjoy seeing my kids grow and, more importantly, play some part in their upbringing? In reality, I knew which way I would choose to go; no contest. My family was, and still is, my life. If I had to leave football in order to spend more time at home, that's what I was prepared to do. After one particularly hectic period, when I hadn't had a day off for five weeks, I spoke with Derek.

'I think I'm done, Derek.'

It took my good friend a while to register what I was saying. At first he thought I meant I was clocking off early for the day. When he realised he was about to lose his closest friend at the club, he sat with me over a coffee and told me why he thought I was making the biggest mistake of my life. I told him my mistake had been coming back into football and not staying in the health service where my friends from university were making progress up the ladder of their careers while working 40-hour weeks with occasional paid overtime at the weekend. Some weeks we were working 70-, 80- or 90-hour weeks. The day I spoke with Derek came at the back end of a particularly gruelling period. We usually alternated away games, but the way the fixtures had fallen, I'd been on duty for a home game at St James' Park on a Saturday, worked on the Sunday rehabbing the injured players and treating the knocks from the game, travelled to Europe on the Monday, returned on the Thursday, travelled with the team on the Friday for the away fixture on the Saturday, then spent a week away with the team for some warm weather training. Derek was now due to travel to the USA with an injured player, which meant I was about to enter into another cycle of home game, Europe, away game, then another away midweek fixture. The commitment required was proving impossible to sustain.

I was exhausted and tearful by the time I raised the issue with Derek. He tried for an hour to talk me around, but to no avail. I couldn't continue to work the way we were required to work. There were only two solutions open to us. Either I left and Derek replaced me with some other poor bastard willing to forego any sort of family life for the sake of a job at Newcastle United, or we employed another member of staff to take a bit of the strain from both of us. Thankfully when we raised the issue with the manager, and then the board, they agreed it was obvious that we needed another member of staff.

It didn't take us long to identify the man we wanted for the job. We'd had many students over the years join us for placements. Our most recent student had completed his successful placement six months previously and was now a newly qualified physiotherapist working at a local hospital. We'd both been impressed with his enthusiasm, dedication and personality, and were convinced he was the man for the job. I had the great pleasure of informing Kevin Bell that we would like him to be employed as the third member of our overworked physiotherapy department. He squealed so loudly with excitement that I had to move the phone from my ear until he'd composed himself enough to finally say yes. Within weeks, to my great relief, he was officially employed as our Academy Physiotherapist, which meant that he would look after the younger players and, more importantly, cover occasional days off for Derek and me. In reality, he spent most of his time assisting us with the senior players.

Kevin had been a mature student and was of a similar age to me. We got on brilliantly as colleagues and he remains a good friend of mine to this day. Softly spoken and dedicated to his craft, he was an instant hit with staff and players alike. A Geordie born and bred, he was also a fanatical Newcastle United fan. I didn't realise quite how fanatical until one particular medical meeting.

I was standing in front of the small gathering. In the room were six or seven key members of staff – physios, doctors, the strength and conditioning coach and the first team coach. Kevin was sitting at the back. He had been in his job for a month or two. I was giving my update on the status of the injured players and their likely availability for the upcoming fixture at the weekend.

'Alan Shearer's thigh strain hasn't improved as quickly as we'd anticipated and he won't be available this weekend. He might be a doubt for the Sunderland game next week –'

My disappointing news was all too much for Kevin. The lifelong Newcastle United fanatic in him, and not the physiotherapist, shouted at me from the back of the room.

'You're fucking joking, aren't you? What have you been doing with him? It's fucking Sunderland next week, man!'

The room fell into eerie silence. Kevin looked around as the stunned faces turned to face him. He raised his hands in apology.

'Sorry, lads. Sorry about that, but it's the Mackems, man . . . I mean . . . wey yee knaa what a mean.'

When the laughter had subsided, I had a quiet word with our newest recruit. I had to remind him that he was in a Newcastle United medical meeting and not in the Strawberry Pub, behind the Gallowgate End, on a match day. I'm not sure he was ever able to fully embrace the point I was making.

That wasn't the last occasion that Kevin Bell the Newcastle United fanatic overpowered Kevin Bell the physiotherapist. The players loved him for it.

I was in the changing room at Old Trafford on 11 April, 1999, when the Newcastle United players were out warming up before our FA Cup semi-final against Tottenham Hotspur. The door burst open and the entire team entered the changing room in fits of laughter and chatter. Gary Speed and Alan Shearer approached me, both eager to speak. Gary got there first.

'You need to go out there and see your mate.'

I was a little confused. Alan Shearer joined in.

'Yes, your mate. Go out and head towards the main stand around the halfway line.'

I took my confusion out of the door, down the long corridor and emerged out of the famous old tunnel in the corner of the Stretford End. The sight and sound of the Newcastle United fans in the main stand nearly took the breath from my lungs. I could feel my whole body tingling as I made my way towards the halfway line. The stand in front of me was rocking up and down under the force of the thousands of jumping Geordies. The noise was deafeningly loud. I still wasn't sure what I was doing walking towards the sea of black and white, but I'm glad I did. It was an incredible sight. I have never seen anything like it before or since at a football match.

I finally reached the touchline at the halfway line. I still wasn't sure what had caused the hilarity in the changing room, or what, or who, I was looking for. I was about to turn and head back when one or two fans began gesticulating to me. They were pointing to someone, or something, in the front row, 10 or 15 metres along from where I was standing. My eyes followed their pointing fingers and immediately settled on the familiar figure who was screaming at the top of his lungs and oblivious to my presence. I walked over to where my physio colleague, Kevin Bell, was swaying. I shouted to him. He didn't register my presence; the brown ale and the occasion had taken him to another place. I stood right in front of him and tried to speak with him. I may as well have been Mike from *The Deer Hunter*, trying to get drug-addled Nick to recognise him in the scene of Russian roulette. Kevin gazed wide-eyed in my general direction. I called out to him. His glassy eyes looked through me and beyond me. He screamed at me and at the world.

Two of the best people I met in all my 18 years at the club. Two inseparable friends, two leaders of men, sharing one of many unforgettable moments. What an image.

'Fuuuuckkkiiing commmonnne! Fuuuuckkkiiing commmonnne!'

Gary Speed was still laughing when I got back to the changing room. He performed a very good impression of Kevin's *fuuuuckkkiiing commmonnne* as well. We won the game 2-0. I like to think Kevin played a small part. He certainly eased the tense atmosphere in the changing room before the game. It proved to be one of the more memorable days in all my time at the club. I hope it was for Kevin too, though I suspect my recollection of events is a little more vivid than his.

Kevin Bell no longer works for Newcastle United. He runs a thriving private practice in the city. He can still be found at St James' Park every home game. He sits somewhere near the halfway line. You might not recognise him at first if you're anywhere in his vicinity, but right before kick-off, just look out for a red-faced, middle-aged man, pumping his fists and screaming *fuuuuckkkiiing commmonnne* several times over into the sky above. That will be Kevin. No wait . . . come to think of it . . . that could be anyone inside St James' Park on any given Saturday.

After the match, Kevin Bell can also be found alongside fellow worshippers in the Trent House Pub. What mood he is in will be entirely dependent on what kind of service he has just experienced in the cathedral of St James' across the road.

'I Put a Spell on You'

Derek Wright, my friend and colleague, was, and still is, a huge Roxy Music fan. Roxy Music caught Derek just at the right moment of his formative years. It was hard for me to envisage, but Derek would regularly regale me with tales of being a teenager, in the front row of Newcastle City Hall, for Roxy Music's iconic gigs in the '70s, dressed head to toe in his full glam-rock attire. Roxy's glory years were a little before my time, so I struggled sometimes to understand his boundless enthusiasm. He was passionately relentless even in the late '90s. I often tried to convert him to the magic of U2, but he'd shake his head dismissively and point out that my favourite band were only great because of the influence of Roxy Music's Brian Eno, who'd helped launch them as a band.

If Derek Wright loved Roxy Music, he absolutely idolised the band's lead singer, Bryan Ferry. We worked with world-famous footballers every day. Derek never paid attention to their fame or fawned over any of them. Their fame and celebrity status were an irrelevance. He treated them as the friends and patients they were. He had a job to do and he didn't let anything get in the way. Nothing or no one fazed Derek Wright. He was always his calm and professional self. Until, that is, the memorable day his boyhood idol Bryan Ferry visited our training complex.

It was the week before the FA Cup Final of 1998. There was a bit of a commotion outside the treatment room, an unusual amount of activity in the hallway, a rush of players clambering the stairs to the canteen. Something was afoot. We had no idea what, but we knew it was something. Stuart Pearce, Derek's good friend and fellow music lover, came rushing into the treatment room.

'Del, Del. You'll never fucking guess who's just strolled in looking a million dollars.'

Derek proved Stuart right by guessing Tony Blair, Robbie Williams, then finally the Spice Girls.

The old punk in Stuart was less than impressed.

'Fuck off, Del . . . the Spice Girls? Why the fuck would the Spice Girls be visiting our training ground . . . and why the fuck d'you think I'd be this excited about it if they did? It's fucking Bryan Ferry! Bryan Ferry's upstairs! Come with me and I'll introduce you to him.'

Stuart, like everyone else at the club, knew just how much Derek loved Roxy Music and Bryan Ferry in particular. It was very kind of him to come down to the treatment room to fetch Bryan's biggest fan so he could go and meet his idol.

There was only one flaw in his plan: Derek flatly refused. Stuart was nonplussed. He shook his head and raised his hands in my direction. By this point, Derek had taken a seat on the treatment table.

'Come on, Derek. It's Bryan Ferry. Get yourself up the stairs and go and meet your idol.'

Derek's flushed cheeks gave me my answer before he spoke. He was shaking from head to toe and jabbering to neither Stuart or to me.

'I, I . . . I just can't. I, I . . . I love him too much. He means too much to me. I can't. I'm sorry, I just can't.'

Stuart rolled his eyes and left us there.

Derek was still stuttering and spluttering when the treatment room door opened and a ridiculously handsome middle-aged man strolled into the cramped treatment room. Derek stopped muttering and stared wide-eyed at Bryan Ferry, as his boyhood idol strutted towards where he was sitting. Bryan flashed my starstruck friend a warm smile and reached out his hand. Derek pulled himself off the treatment table. Bryan spoke.

'You must be Derek. Stuart's been telling me all about you. I didn't want to leave without coming to say hello.'

Derek was unsteady on his feet. I thought he might collapse back onto the bed. He reached out his hand and shook the hand of his idol. Then he shook it – and shook it again. There came a moment when, by all the conventions of normal etiquette, this one should have come to its natural end. The moment passed. I recognised it, Stuart Pearce recognised it, Bryan Ferry certainly recognised it. Derek Wright? He was oblivious. He just kept on shaking like he would never let go. What seemed like an eternity passed as Derek held onto Bryan's hand and stared into his eyes. Stuart looked at me and looked at Derek, locked onto Bryan. He nodded for me to intervene. So I did.

'You can let go of his hand now, Derek.'

He didn't do so immediately, but I'd broken the spell. He softened his grip and Bryan slid his hand into the safety of his pocket. Bryan was warm and gracious. He spent some time sitting on the treatment couch chatting with us. We had our photo taken with him. He was 20 years older than me, but he looked 10 years younger.

Bryan Ferry was fantastic with Derek that day. Just as an idol should be when confronted by such a devoted disciple. But there was more to come from him. Much more. On the evening of our FA Cup Final defeat, Bryan Ferry came to our table at dinner. He pulled up a chair next to Derek Wright and spent time chatting with him like he was an old friend.

Three years later, I was with Derek as we sat in the sixth row of a Bryan Ferry concert, at the City Hall in Newcastle. The great man came on stage looking effortlessly cool as always. He was singing 'I Put a Spell on You'. In the middle of the song, Bryan put his hand on his forehead and scanned the audience. Then he found the man he was looking for. Beaming a wide smile, he gave Derek Wright a thumbs up. Derek hit me so hard with his elbow I thought he'd broken my ribs.

'Did you see that, Paul? Did you see that man? Fuck me! Did you see that?'

I rubbed my hand across my bruised ribs. I was so pleased to see my great friend so happy in that moment.

'Yes, Derek, I saw it. I saw it.'

They say you should never meet your idols. Probably for a good reason in many cases, I'm sure, but Bryan Ferry was incredibly gracious with the middle-aged Derek Wright who'd idolised him as a 14-year-old glam rocker screaming from the front row of the City Hall in Newcastle all those years before.

Well played, Bryan. You certainly put a spell on him.

A Cup final - and a prized possession

After back-to-back second place finishes in the Premier League in 1996 and 1997, Newcastle United limped to a disappointing 13th place finish in 1998. It was quite the fall from the dizzy heights of the previous two campaigns. The seeds were sown at the very beginning of the season when the club made the decision to break up the phenomenally successful Shearer/Ferdinand partnership and offered Les to Spurs. Before the deal could be completed, Alan Shearer suffered an horrific fracture dislocation of his ankle in a preseason game at Goodison Park. Frantic efforts were made to abort the Ferdinand transfer, but to no avail. The potent team of 1997, with Ferdinand and Shearer at the helm, was effectively toothless for the first half of the new season. Alan worked diligently to get himself fit from his devastating injury. It was the honour of my professional life as a physiotherapist to share that journey and he returned to the team for the fourth round of the FA Cup.

Despite continued poor League form, Newcastle United made it all the way to the Cup final. The club's first Cup final since Dennis Tueart had broken Kieran Moran's heart in the League Cup final of 1976. Even as a physio, it was a great thrill to be involved in such an iconic occasion. Leaving the team hotel, as the BBC helicopter flew overhead and filmed our coach journey to Wembley, took me right back to those Cup final days as a boy, when I'd sit glued to the TV from the early morning of the game. I loved the build-up as much as the game itself. 1998 was no different. Driving up Wembley Way, past hordes of delirious Newcastle fans, exiting the coach to their deafening roar, strolling onto the Wembley turf in the blazing sunshine – it was all magical, and I was merely a physiotherapist.

Just before kick-off, I slipped out of the changing room and stood at the edge of the tunnel. I thought my chest was about to explode as I listened to the whole stadium sing 'Abide with Me'. In 1998, I shared on-field match-day duties with Derek Wright. Today, it was his turn. There was no room on the bench at Wembley, so when we had completed our tasks in the changing room, I joined kitman Ray Thompson in the royal box. Arsenal fan Mick Jagger was our neighbour for the day. The excitement and anticipation just before kick-off was like nothing I've ever experienced before. A feeling of *This is it. This is our day. This is our destiny.* Then Marc Overmars gave Arsenal the lead in a first half they dominated and it started to feel like maybe it was Arsenal's destiny after all. Newcastle started brightly in the second half. Nikos Dabizas hit the bar before Alan Shearer fired a shot off the post. But Arsenal scored a second through Nicolas Anelka, and that was that.

We left a smiling Mick Jagger in the royal box, walked past the FA Cup trophy as it was being decorated in the red and white ribbons of Arsenal, and made our way into the changing room no one wants to visit. The losers changing room at Wembley is a desolate place to be. No one spoke. What was there to say? I kept my head down, and attended to the cuts and bruises of defeat. I was glad when it was finally time to leave the stifling atmosphere of the changing room. As I reached the door, I felt something brush the back of my leg. I looked down to see a match-worn shirt on the floor. I picked it up and read the name Shearer on the back. I looked across to where Alan was sitting. He raised his thumb to me. I shrugged my shoulders and brought his shirt back to him. He shook his head.

'I don't want it. I want you to have it, for all the help you've given me, getting me back.'

I took the shirt home and kept it safe over the summer. On the first day of preseason training, I handed it back to Alan,

'That's your Cup final shirt. You should have it. It was all a bit emotional on the day, but you shouldn't give away your Cup final shirt.'

He took it from me and thanked me. I was glad to give it back to its rightful owner, but also a little disappointed. Two weeks later, Alan walked into the treatment room, carrying a huge frame. Inside that frame was his Cup final shirt. There was a photo of the moment he hit the post. On the photo was a personal message of thanks for the work I'd done in helping him through a difficult period in his illustrious career. It was a fine gesture. The framed Cup final shirt still hangs proudly in my home to this day.

El Gordo and El Gordito

There are certain players who come into a football club and just light the place up with their character and personality. When Peruvian international Nobby Solano joined us from Boca Juniors in 1998, it was very obvious to everyone who met him that he was just such a character. He would go on to make me and many others laugh every day we worked with him. I still smile now when I think of his personality and charisma in and around the dressing room. He was warm, engaging and funny. He also had a bit of devilment in him. I established that from my first encounter.

It was very clear to me he was up for a joke and a laugh, even at his own expense. I knew I was on safe ground when I instructed him, as part of his medical examination, to wait in the treatment room because there was something very pressing and of great concern that I needed to discuss with my colleague, Derek Wright. Nobby looked a little confused but agreed. I found Derek in the canteen and he followed me back to the treatment room. We wore our most stern faces as we entered the room.

I brought Derek over to where Nobby was sitting patiently. We didn't smile as we stood staring intently at Newcastle United's latest signing. Derek rubbed his chin and shook his head as I pointed at Nobby.

'Derek, this fella's passport states that he is only twenty-three years old.'

I raised my palms.

'D'you think he's twenty-three?'

Derek pointed at Nobby and looked at me.

'No fucking way, Paul. No way is that old fella twenty-three. Thirty-three at a push I'd say.'

We leaned forward in unison so we were right next to Nobby's face. He sat for a brief moment, his eyes flicking between mine and Derek's. He flashed us a wide smile and climbed to his feet. He was wagging his finger as he pushed past us.

'Ah. I see, my friends, the physios at Newcastle are bastardos. I see this now.'

We laughed and shook hands, but it was our Peruvian friend who had the last laugh.

'My friends, this is war. From this day forward you two jokers shall be known as *El Gordo* (the fat one) and *El Gordito* (little fatty).'

Nobby kept his word and never called us by our names for the rest of his time at the club. We were indeed *El Gordo* and *El Gordito* from that day forward. I have many happy memories of the people I met in my 18-year odyssey with Newcastle United. None have made me smile more than the young Peruvian with the old face and amazing personality. I even miss being woken in the middle of the night by my phone buzzing on the bedside table. I'd recognise the number. I knew what was coming before I answered, but I always answered. Then I'd be forced to listen to Nobby Solano play his trumpet for what seemed like an eternity until he hung up and called someone else to annoy.

Even the great Bobby Robson wasn't immune from a late-night phone call and trumpet session. The ageing manager, who'd seen it all in football, burst into the treatment room one morning. He was full of fake fury and indignation.

'Where is he? The bloody idiot with the trumpet? Had me up half the bloody night he did. The temerity of that bloody nuisance waking his manager up in the middle of the night. It's unbelievable . . .'

Bobby was still ranting when the sound of Nobby's trumpet came blaring down the hall and drowned out his protestations.

The manager stopped, shook his head and smiled. He turned to me and Derek.

'The game needs more characters like that, boys. He's a one-off, isn't he? He's also lucky he can play a bit. I wouldn't be having that if he was shit, I can tell you.'

Listening to the many bum notes Nobby was hitting, it was clear Bobby was referring to his football ability and not his musical talent.

One of the great pleasures of working within professional football was the opportunity it gave me to meet and befriend people from different cultures and backgrounds from all over the world. Nolberto Albino Solano Todco was an incredibly gifted footballer and a beautiful human being. When I think back to both of his spells at the club I can't help but do so with a smile. I also can't help but wonder how old he actually is now. He must be in his early sixties, surely?

Nobby Solano strikes for goal in 2001. One of the most naturally gifted footballers I ever had the pleasure of working with. One of the finest characters too.

'They don't eat the green sweets...'

Goals from Alan Shearer and Gary Speed guaranteed Newcastle United emerged victorious from our third round FA Cup tie against Crystal Palace on 2 January, 1999. Just as well, because a defeat would have ruined a trip to Glasgow which a small group of us had planned. The win ensured we were all in good spirits as we made our way out of the stadium, on the official team coach. We were off for a two-night break in Scotland. The main purpose was to experience the thrills and excitement of the Old Firm derby – the match between Rangers and Celtic – at Ibrox Stadium. Our group was comprised of players and backroom staff, and included Alan Shearer, Gary Speed, Shay Given and Steve Harper. We filled the coach with alcohol and enjoyed a boozy three-hour journey north.

In the magnificent city of Glasgow, we had a great night before stumbling back to our hotel in the early hours of the morning. I shared a room with Alan Shearer and we spent most of the weekend in each other's company. The only exception was on the day of the game. We were together in the morning, but as we left our city centre hotel, and made our way towards the famous old stadium, everything changed. In order for us to enjoy the game safely we had to be segregated two hours before kick-off and for two hours after it as well.

We were forced to part because most of us (me included) were due to experience the famous atmosphere from the away end. This wasn't because the players and staff at Newcastle United were fanatical Glasgow Celtic fans, but rather because our tickets for the match came courtesy of our former club doctor, who was now Celtic's club doctor. Glasgow Rangers had been informed that Alan Shearer was intending to watch the game and very kindly provided two tickets for the directors box for Alan and a friend. So we said our goodbyes to Alan and Gary Speed, who'd agreed to slum it with Alan in the directors box. The security cordon that surrounded us that day as we made our way towards Ibrox was like nothing I'd ever experienced before in football and like nothing I've experienced since. Police wagons and police officers were everywhere along the route. It was an incredible security operation for just one football match. I found it unnerving, intimidating and far from enjoyable. It was ugly, hostile and surreal. I would happily have turned around and gone back to the hotel.

The match itself proved to be one of the strangest experiences I've ever had at a football match. We linked up with some Celtic fans inside a dingy pub close to Ibrox. It was a swaying, noisy, sea of green and white. We somehow managed to get a drink and stood in a corner, squashed between a jukebox and a slot machine. One of the strangers next to me, dressed head to toe in green and white, asked me my name. I shouted over the Pogues belting out 'Sally MacLennane', that my name was Paul Ferris. The stranger instantly recognised the name. His jaw dropped and his drink nearly dropped too. He shouted to me again just to make sure he'd heard me properly. Twice more I told him I was Paul Ferris before he was finally satisfied. He disappeared and weaved his way to the bar. I saw him talking animatedly to a group of friends. They were waving at me. So I waved back. Then they cheered me loudly and began singing and pointing their collective fingers in my direction. By the time their voices had reached my ears, the whole heaving mass of green and white was singing along with them. The entire pub was facing me and singing my name. They chanted to the melody of 'Guantanamera':

Two Paul Ferrises,
There's only two Paul Ferrises.
Two Paul Ferrises,
There's only two Paul Ferrises . . .

Apparently I shared my name with an extremely well-known Glasgow underworld figure, who also just happened to be a diehard Celtic fan.

When we reached the stadium, and took up our position behind the goal, the atmosphere was breathtaking. Loud, incessant and hostile. The game was average, but the game didn't matter. The atmosphere was everything. It was white-hot. I was glad when the half-time whistle blew.

I was bursting for the bathroom and ready for my first bit of solid food of the day. As I was making my way past a couple of Celtic fans, one of them put his hand across my chest and stopped me in my tracks.

'Where are you going, wee man?'

I was bit startled.

'Ah. . . I'm going to the toilet and then maybe to get a burger or a pie or something.'

He kept his hand on my chest and relayed my reply to his mates.

'Here, boys . . . he says he's going to get some food. Have you ever heard the like of it?'

His mates were shaking their heads and laughing in my direction. I was totally perplexed. I looked at his hand that was still firmly on my chest.

'Is there a problem with that?'

He turned to his mates.

'He says, is there a problem with that?'

They laughed again, I had no idea whatsoever why what I was saying was in any way funny.

I moved his hand.

'Sorry, I don't understand. I'm just going to get some food.'

He put his hand back on my chest and his tone hardened.

'Like fuck you are, wee man. You're not giving these orange bastards a penny of your money. You should've eaten something before you came into this shithole. You can go for a piss, but that's it. Nae fuckin food, d'you hear?'

I couldn't believe what he was saying, but it was crystal clear he meant every word.

I didn't get my food. I had my piss. I walked past the deserted concession stand on the concourse, then watched the rest of match with a rumbling belly and a sense of disbelief at the levels of bigotry and sectarianism surrounding me. I was starving when I got back to my hotel room hours later. Alan Shearer was already there. I couldn't wait to tell him about the nonsense I'd experienced regarding buying food at Ibrox. Alan laughed and cut me off mid-sentence.

'You think that's bad. I can better that, man. They were handing around wine gums in the Rangers' directors box. By the time they came to me, there were only green ones left. I asked one of the directors why there were only green ones left. He said none of them would eat the green shite. Fuck me, man . . . they don't eat the green sweets! How fucking mad is that?'

It was mad. Totally mad. All of it. I'm not sure I enjoyed my experience of the Celtic/Rangers game. There's no doubt the atmosphere was incredible. But it was also hate-filled and ugly. It reminded me too much of the bollox I'd endured as a child growing up during the Troubles.

The game itself improved in the second half. I would've just preferred watching it with a little less bigotry.

As for the other Paul Ferris, I looked him up. He's a reformed character who writes books now. It transpires that we were both living in the north-east of England at the same time in the 1990s. I was living in the beautiful village of Horsley in Northumberland. He was living in the not so beautiful HM Prison Frankland. There's only two Paul Ferrises.

Ruining Gazza's diet

Testimonials were still a prominent feature of the football landscape in the late '90s. Today it seems like they've all but disappeared. Gone are the days of the stalwart footballer who spends 10 or 15 years at the same club, then enjoys a rousing send-off and a well-deserved payday before carrying his bulging saddlebags off into a comfortable retirement. Testimonials may well still be prevalent lower down the footballing pyramid, but they no longer have a significant part to play in elite football. Maybe players at the top level simply don't hang around at one club for long enough anymore. The globalisation of the game and the influx of expensive foreign players, who stay for three or four years before taking their young families back home, is certainly a factor. The more likely reason for the demise of the testimonial is that players at the elite level now earn such vast sums of money that yet another boost to their coffers seems more like an obscenity than a thank you for loyal service. Testimonials do still take place occasionally. Thankfully, the recipients in most instances have the good sense to donate the proceeds to worthy causes. They get their final moment in the sun, where the fans can thank them for their years of sterling service, and some worthy cause in the local community benefits from the funds generated.

When they were still all the rage, I used to look forward to testimonials. They were always very enjoyable. The atmosphere in the dressing room was very relaxed and completely different from the normal intensity and edginess that was ever-present for competitive matches. Testimonials were always an occasion to reconnect with old friends and colleagues who hadn't been around since they'd left the club many years before. They were also an opportunity to meet a footballing great from another club or another era. Peter Beardsley's testimonial, on 27 January, 1999, was memorable. Many old players and old friends from the past spent time relaxing in the treatment room, reminiscing about times gone by and where life had taken them since they'd last played at St James' Park. Paul Gascoigne was among them. He was playing for Middlesborough at the time, and back living in the north-east, but our paths hadn't crossed since the day I'd met him in Rome when I'd visited Lazio in 1995. It was always a pleasure to catch up with him. He was a ball of mischievous energy every time we met. That night was no different. Before the game, he was as warm, cheeky and friendly as ever. I did notice he had a swollen lip, but he assured me it was nothing to be concerned about.

'Divvent worry about that Ferra, man. It's just a bit of snus.'

I'd no idea what he was talking about. He could tell as much by the look of confusion on my face. He pulled his lip from his gum to show me the little pouch trapped in between.

'It's tobacco, man. One of the Rangers boys from Scandinavia got me into it. It's fucking mint, man. Helps us relax an aal that. D'you wanna try some?'

Paul Gascoigne, taking early steps to the stratosphere, at St James' Park, in April 1987.

I politely declined. The game kicked off. It was a typical testimonial, played at a snail's pace, and featuring current and past Newcastle United superstars chasing the shadows of the current Celtic team around St James' Park. It was a very mundane evening for me, until I noticed Gazza was looking more than a little unsteady on his feet. I wasn't sure if my mind was playing tricks. I stopped watching the game and kept my eyes firmly fixed on my former teammate. When I was sure I wasn't imagining things, I tapped Kevin Keegan on the shoulder. Kevin was managing Newcastle United for the occasion. Gazza stumbled and swayed in front of us as the game played out around him. Kevin agreed Gazza should come off and he took his place on the field to rapturous applause and familiar chants of 'Keegan, Keegan, Keegan'.

Paul was unsteady as I walked him straight down the tunnel. We'd barely got out of sight of the packed arena before his wobbly legs gave way. He collapsed onto me and we fell against the tunnel wall. I shouted back into the cauldron as I tried to hold him up. A masseur came to our aid. We carried Gazza into the treatment room and laid him on the couch. He was semi-conscious and very weak, but able to ask me for a drink and a sandwich. He scoffed the sandwich and guzzled the drink. He asked for another sandwich. The food and drink acted as a miracle cure. Within minutes he was sitting upright, smiling and munching on a third sandwich. I was pleased and relieved to see him back to his old self. It quickly became clear Gazza wasn't so pleased. He looked at his empty drink sachet in one hand and the remainder of his third sandwich in the other. He threw them both on the floor like they were poison.

'Fuck's sake, Ferra man. What have you done? You've ruined me fuckin diet, man!'

I laughed. He didn't. I apologised.

'I'm sorry. I didn't know you were on a diet. Anyway, you're a professional footballer. You don't need to be on a diet.'

I asked him what he'd eaten that day.

'Eaten? I've eaten nowt, man! I've just been drinking water with a bit of honey and lemon in it! Now you've ruined it!'

I delved a bit deeper. He'd been starving himself for the previous three days. It's a miracle he was able to run at all, never mind last 75 minutes. I spent the next 15 minutes trying to convince him to resume a sensible eating plan immediately. He put some snus between his lip and gums and ignored every word I said. I was glad I'd sabotaged his diet. Even if it was for one night only.

'There's always someone with a bigger boat!'

Two days after Newcastle United's 1999 FA Cup final defeat to Manchester United, we embarked on our first foreign holiday as a young family. We arrived at our apartment block in Menorca in the middle of the night and walked straight into an all-night party that was in full swing and spilling out of the neighbouring apartment across the balcony, blocking the doorway to our apartment. The intoxicated kids we pushed our way through were all very pleasant. And very excited to hear our Irish accents. One half-dressed young girl with a thick Belfast accent offered to share her half-drunk bottle of Buckfast.

'What about the wee ones? Would they like a wee sip? It'll help them sleep.'

We politely declined. We were glad to get our seven-year-old son, Conor, and our two-year-old toddler, Owen, into the sanctuary of our accommodation. We put them to bed and climbed into ours. We lay there for an hour or two. The party got louder as the Buckfast worked its magic on the crowd of lively teenagers crowded around our door. It was a rude welcome to our first trip abroad. The thought of spending 14 nights listening to 'The Fields of Athenry' being murdered on each and every one of those nights, ensured we were soon discussing alternative options.

The window of the apartment didn't close properly, so we were joined by a mosquito who feasted on both of us while we tried to get some much-needed sleep as the morning sun blazed its way through the curtainless window. That was the deal-breaker. That morning, I walked wearily to a local estate agent and spent several hours in a public phone booth calling other agents in an attempt to find us alternative accommodation to avoid us having to endure the holiday from hell. My perseverance paid off. Three hours into my quest, we were offered a place to rent for the next 13 days at a ridiculously low rate. I think the lovely woman who offered it could hear the desperation in my voice and took pity.

We moved into a beautiful villa in Fornells for the rest of our holiday. It was a very well appointed three-bedroom villa with a private pool, set in a beautiful part of the island. It would've been way beyond our budget without the kindness of the letting agent. We were still ecstatic as we wandered around the picturesque village. We turned a corner and I heard a familiar voice call out to me.

'What are you doing on my island, Mr Ferris?'

John Barnes was smiling at me as he crossed the road. He had departed from Newcastle United that February after a short stint with us. It was an unexpected pleasure to see him again. Such is the nature of professional football I hadn't really had the chance to say a proper goodbye. He was undoubtedly one of the most engaging, articulate and genuinely warm characters I'd ever come across in football. And an incredibly intelligent man. He'd come into the treatment room every day and we'd debate and argue the big issues of the day. That didn't happen very often at Newcastle United in the late '90s! I was disappointed when he left.

In a small seafront café in Fornells, we spent 10 minutes chatting about football, the best restaurants in the area, and his future plans for a managerial career he was very keen to embark upon. We readied to leave and said our goodbyes. I thought that would be the end of our contact in Menorca and the last I would ever see of him. John Barnes had other ideas. He tapped my arm as I was making my way to the door.

'What are you doing tomorrow?'

I told him we'd just arrived and had no plans.

'Be on the beach at 10 a.m. I have a little surprise for you and the family.'

We reported to the beach as instructed. John was nowhere to be seen. We walked up and down the long stretch of golden sand, dragging our reluctant kids and all their belongings with us. We got a few strange looks from confused strangers on sun loungers as we passed by them for the fifth time. The sweat was stinging my eyes and the kids were baked. We decided the best thing to do was to head back to our villa. I had one last look along the beach but saw no sign of John. Then I looked out to sea and saw a boat on the horizon. It was making its way at some speed towards the shore and to where we were standing. It wasn't a big boat by any means. Maybe 20 feet long and with a jet ski attached. As it approached, I could see John Barnes waving at us, beckoning us to the water's edge. A proud Captain Barnes climbed off his boat, then waded through the water until his feet found dry land. Murmuring holiday-makers chattered and pointed as the former England superstar led my young family off the beach into the water, towards his boat. We climbed the ladder and joined his young family on board. Twenty minutes later, we were drinking champagne and picnicking on our own private beach. John gave my kids rides on the jet ski. It was an amazing day – far removed from our everyday lives and a very different holiday experience to our first night spent flirting with Buckfast and mosquitoes.

We'd been there for an hour or two when into our private cove came a huge sunseeker yacht. Two jet skis made their way towards us from the back of the yacht. John and I walked to the water's edge and greeted our friendly intruders. Two familiar faces hopped off the jet skis and shook our hands. Eddie Jordan, the Formula 1 racing team owner, and Paul McGinley, the professional golfer, then spent an hour chatting and playing with the kids. They were gracious and charming – and as excited to meet John Barnes as he was to meet them. Eddie invited us onto his yacht for dinner. It would've been an amazing experience, and I was a little surprised when John politely declined. Instead we said our goodbyes. As Eddie Jordan and Paul McGinley sped off on their jet skis, John shook his head.

'Isn't that fucking typical! Here I am, showing off my boat to you, then a fucking superyacht turns up! I'm telling you, no matter how well you think you're doing in life, there's always someone with a bigger boat!'

The light faded and we boarded John's boat. We left the calmness of the cove. The weather changed, the waters rose, and the 10-minute journey back to the original beach took us nearly an hour and a half. Waves were lapping over the sides of John's small boat, and at times we felt like we weren't moving anywhere. The kids were crying, we were freezing and I don't mind admitting I was more than a little terrified that we were never going to make it back to shore.

I am still extremely grateful for John Barnes' wonderful hospitality that day, but I've never been so relieved to find my feet on dry land. I don't suppose Eddie Jordan's bigger boat had quite the same difficulties we had, John?

A book signing

The late, and most certainly great, Sir Bobby Robson was the best manager I worked with as a player or physio. From the day he arrived, in September 1999 until the day he left in 2004, he was simply a pleasure to be around. I spent hours in conversation with him alongside my colleague Derek Wright. Because of the configuration of our training ground, Bobby could take a shortcut to the front door by walking through the treatment room. Every day after the players and staff had departed, the treatment room door would open gently, but instead of passing through Sir Bobby would climb onto a treatment couch. He always led with the same question.

'Don't suppose there's a quick cup of tea going, boys?'

Most days that quick cup of tea led to another, and another after that. He talked about his family, our families, his career, our careers, the players, football, the north-east, Ireland and everything and anything else that came into his head. I didn't really appreciate it at the time, but what a privilege those days were for me and Derek. I look back on them now with great fondness.

Bobby was a lovely man as well as a footballing great. Brimming with charm and charisma. He was encyclopaedic in his knowledge of football and he was an expert at managing what was, at the time, quite a difficult group of players. He was also prone to a gaffe or two that made working alongside him always entertaining. He hadn't been long in the job when word came back to the club of a recent book signing event Bobby had attended. A friend of Alan Shearer's had queued for hours in Waterstones to meet Bobby and get the former England manager's signature on his newly purchased book. Alan's mate eventually reached the front of the hour-long queue. He was naturally thrilled to meet his idol and sought to prolong this once-in-a-lifetime encounter. He therefore made some small talk with a now very tired, but still charmingly accommodating, Bobby Robson. Alan's friend sympathised with the great man as he asked him to dedicate the book to his son Peter.

'You must be very tired, Bobby, signing all these books.'

Bobby raised his eyebrows and nodded wearily in agreement as he signed the title page of the book.

'I'm bloody exhausted, son. I must've signed hundreds of these books today. Hundreds of them. Don't get me wrong, it's bloody fantastic, but I'm getting far too old for this, you know.'

He handed the book back to Alan's friend. They posed for a photo together, before Bobby shook his hand warmly and ushered the excited fan on his way.

As soon as Alan's Shearer's friend got home, he took his spoils from the bag to show his uninterested wife the great man's signature. His wife agreed that their Newcastle United-mad son would be overjoyed with this personalised Christmas gift from Sir Bobby Robson.

As he turned the pages and found the signed title page, there was a moment of stunned silence as the pair digested the words on the page in front of them. Then in unison they filled their kitchen with laughter. The simple dedication read:

To Peter,
Best Wishes,
Bobby Hundreds

Well, Bobby did say he was tired. Peter never did get his book signed 'Bobby Robson'. I like to think he got something a hundred times better.

'Wait until you hear him sing!'

Gary Speed loved his music. I've always loved my music. We bonded as friends over our shared love of music. We'd regularly exchange CDs of the latest bands we'd discovered. He introduced me to music I'd never heard before and I did the same for him. Gary was a handsome man, an intelligent man, a good man – and more. He excelled at everything he turned his hand to, and that included playing the guitar. Very soon after purchasing the thing, he became more than proficient. He could really play.

I regarded Gary as much more than just a footballer I happened to work alongside. He was one of the very few players I regarded as a close friend. We socialised together, sat together on long coach journeys around the country, were part of what just might have been the most competitive Trivial Pursuit competition in history. I'd partner with the club doctor to take on Gary and Steve Harper on every away trip. It was great for relieving the boredom of a four-hour journey down the road.

The game was usually played in good spirits, but to the embarrassment of all four of us it sometimes descended into acrimonious farce when competitive instincts trumped common sense. On more than one occasion the board flew into the air, scattering the wedges all over the luxury coach. Playing board games with professional sportsmen is not recommended. They're just too competitive for their own good. Gary was a fierce competitor. He wanted to win at everything. He had to be the fittest player in preseason. His body fat statistics had to be the best of the group. He was a horrible loser on match day and took the greatest joy in victory. He was also a pleasure to rehab from the one or two injuries he sustained while at Newcastle United.

I learned one rainy day, though, never to compete when rehabbing him. I won our game of head tennis and raised my hand in victory. He ran around the net and berated me for 10 minutes as to why I should concentrate more on getting him fit than trying to beat him at head tennis. He really was a bad loser – which is part of what made him a great footballer. The cup of tea and the biscuit he brought into the treatment room, alongside his sincere apology for losing his temper, was what made him a great man. He was complex in many ways, but in other ways a simple man. He loved his family, his football and his life.

In June 2011, I spent a week with him in Barbados. We were there as part of the Newcastle United team, taking part in a footballing legends invitational tournament. I was there very much not as a legend, but because Alan Shearer had invited me as he was contemplating a managerial role at Cardiff City and we needed to compile a report on how to approach it. Gary was the manager of Wales at the time. Unsurprisingly, he was making a brilliant success of that job too. He wasn't his usual bubbly self on the trip, though, and I told him so over breakfast. He confided that he was having some personal issues, but he was adamant he had them under control and was dealing with them. We parted with a promise to keep in touch more. In truth, I've never been very good at the whole keeping in touch thing. So, instead, I watched from afar as he continued to thrive as his country's footballing Messiah. Then one Sunday morning in November 2011 I received a call from Alan Shearer. He spoke two words.

'Speedo's dead.'

It took a moment for me to register what he'd said. I felt my legs begin to shake. I slumped onto the couch. Alan spoke again.

'You still there?'

'Yes. I'm still here. I don't understand. Was he in an accident?'

Alan's response ensured the rest of my body followed my legs. I hung up. I was home alone. I cried.

Back in 2000, Gary was bursting with life. He was young, handsome, famous, and the world was his for the taking. I think about his laughter, his goals, his talent. I think about him learning to play the guitar and his impressive dedication to his latest passion.

Every afternoon, when the other players had gone home, he'd fetch his prized guitar from the car and play me a gig in the treatment room. I'm not sure if it was because he knew I liked the music, or because he knew I was a captive audience. I don't know who his tutor was, but Gary seemed to go from novice to finger-picking expert almost overnight. He loved the Stereophonics and fancied himself as the next Kelly Jones, the lead singer of the Welsh band. I loved almost everything about those afternoons when Gary Speed would bring his guitar and sing. Almost everything.

We were at a party at Rob Lee's house in Durham. We were always at a party at Rob Lee's house in Durham. Geraldine and I were sitting in one of the many rooms of Rob's beautiful home. We were having a quiet drink, away from the noise and madness of the main party. Gary popped his head around the door.

'D'you mind if I play my guitar? Nobody in there wants to listen.'

I looked at Geraldine. She nodded her approval. He strutted in, guitar in hand, looking every inch the glamorous footballer that he was. He lifted his leg up onto the chair. He positioned his guitar, like he was Elvis Presley in the *1968 Comeback Special*. Then he began effortlessly finger-picking the instantly recognisable introduction to the Stereophonics' 'Just Looking'.

Geraldine shuffled in her chair. She nudged me.

'He's bloody fantastic.'

Gary played on, oblivious to our conversation. After months of listening to him play, I knew what was coming. I whispered to her.

'Wait until you hear him sing!'

She didn't have to wait long before Gary sang the opening lines.

There's things I want . . .

I said nothing. Geraldine nudged me again.

'Bloody hell. He's really awful, isn't he?'

I whispered back.

'Don't I know it. I've had to listen to that every day for the past eight months.'

Gary Speed was undoubtedly a handsome man. Gary Speed was clearly an intelligent man. Gary Speed was unequivocally a good man, but JESUS CHRIST, he was one dreadful singer! I had to listen to him on several more occasions after that night before he departed for Bolton Wanderers. His most public appearance as a crooner was on the coach on the way home from a U2 Concert in Glasgow, in 2001. Everyone, apart from me, was fast asleep. By the time Gary had finished murdering his version of 'One', I wished I'd been asleep as well. Great man, great footballer, great guitar player. His singing? Irrefutable evidence that not all Welshmen were born to sing!

A stray testicle, a tough Geordie and a convention of nuns

In March 2001, I accompanied Alan Shearer on his career-saving visit to Colorado. It was the third time visiting Dr Richard Steadman, the world-renowned knee surgeon. As we boarded our plane, the captain was at the door to great us. A discreet 'Mr Shearer, please follow me', and we were on our way to an upgraded seat. It was the first time in my life I'd flown first class. I thanked Alan for his celebrity status and settled down with a glass of wine or three and a film. On Alan's recommendation, I watched the brilliantly funny *Purely Belter* - a poignant and hilarious tale of two Geordie boys down on their luck who embark on a quest to purchase two season tickets to watch their beloved Newcastle United. My enjoyment of the film was only slightly impaired by Alan nudging me at all of the key moments. He'd seen it twice before.

'Watch this bit, man, it's bloody fantastic!'

He was oblivious to the fact he was shouting while wearing headphones and that I could barely hear him anyway because of the matching headphones I was wearing. When the film ended, I drank more wine as I read my book under the bright reading light in the dimmed cabin.

I've never worn underpants as an adult. That seems a strange admission to make at this point, I know, but it is very relevant to the turn of events that followed. The wine ensured I fell asleep only minutes into reading my book. I tossed and turned in the narrow bed before I eventually awoke again some hours later with the reading light still illuminating my individual pod. The effects of the wine, the sleep and the alien environment meant it took me a moment or two to fully gather my senses. I was lying on my back with my legs wide apart and bent at the knees. I became aware of a draft of cold air between my legs. I raised my head and peeped down. I wish I hadn't. I could see a pale oval object where the seam of my trousers should have been. The seam had torn just a little.

Just a little, but big enough to enable my right testicle to escape. It was now perched proudly outside my trousers for the whole world to see. How long had the little bastard been there? I'll never know. But there it was all the same. A perfect little sphere freed from its prison beneath my inadequate trousers. I was horrified. Quickly I slid my hand down and poked the offending protuberance back inside the tear in my useless trousers. I didn't dare to look up as I was performing this deft manoeuvre. I'm very glad I didn't. When I eventually did, I couldn't miss the female member of the cabin crew standing right in my eyeline. She had an unobstructed view to the place in my lap where my testicle used to be. I smiled at her. She averted her gaze. Wouldn't you? Wouldn't anybody? Who smiles at a stranger in the immediate aftermath of pushing a testicle back inside their trousers? She didn't smile back. Instead she behaved as if she hadn't seen my testicle. I knew she'd seen it. I tried to behave as if she hadn't. She tried to behave as if she hadn't. She most definitely had. In truth, it had probably been out there long enough for her to identify it in a line-up with five other suspects. I couldn't wait to get off the flight. I suspect the feeling was mutual for her too.

We were still laughing about my errant testicle when we arrived at our ski resort hotel in beautiful Vail. It was very remote and we were off season, the only guests. I reached the grand reception desk before Alan and enquired about our rooms.

'We have two rooms booked. One for Mr Shearer and one for Mr Ferris.'

Before the pleasant receptionist had time to reply, a voice boomed from over my shoulder.

'Mr Shearer and Mr Ferris will be sharing a room.'

I was a little confused and asked Alan why.

'Because I'm afraid of the dark, man.'

This was a surprising, but welcome admission, for me to hear. I too am afraid of the dark – and have been all of my life.

Alan Shearer was in the recovery room following his successful surgery. I was sitting by his bed. He was on a morphine drip for pain relief. He hadn't quite come around and was still a little drowsy. He began groaning. The concerned American nurse spoke to him.

'Would you like some more pain relief, Alan?'

He shook his head and mumbled an answer. The caring nurse didn't understand. I did. It made me smile. She asked him again if he required any extra pain relief. This time she heard him loud and clear, but she still didn't understand. Through his drug-induced fog, in his thick Geordie accent, he'd replied:

'I'm a Geordie, man. I'm a Geordie.'

She looked to me with her arms raised and palms facing the sky. I translated Alan's reply:

'He says he's from a tough part of the world and therefore he doesn't require any extra pain relief!'

Because Alan wasn't able to get up and about and wasn't permitted to travel post-surgery, we spent 10 days locked in our room. By the eighth day we were getting very restless. We agreed I'd go down to the bar and bring back some beers. I was excited just to be out of the room. The entire hotel was deserted and bathed in an eerie silence; there wasn't a guest or ghost in sight. I ordered six bottles of Budweiser from the lonely bartender at the quiet hotel bar. As I turned with my spoils to make my way to the elevator, I was met by a flock of a hundred nuns dressed in full habits. I stood wide-eyed and open-mouthed as the throng serenely glided past reception and gathered at the elevator doors. *Where the fuck did they come from? A flock of nuns?*

'What are you wearing for the FA Cup semi-final? Just your trousers? No bother. Me too. Belter.' Newcastle United fans at Wembley in 2000.

Really? I stared at them for a brief moment. Then I stared at my hands and pockets full of the devil's brew. Or, in my case, Budweiser.

I was suddenly overcome with shame and embarrassment to be loaded up on beers in front of so many brides of Christ. I had to think fast. I could empty my pockets and hands and head nonchalantly towards the elevator and the gathered congregation, or I could keep hold of my beer, bolt up the stairs, catch the elevator on the first floor and ferry my devil's brew up to our tenth-floor room before they'd even crammed their way through the elevator doors on the ground floor. Seemed like a good plan. I raced up the stairs. Beer spilled over my trousers and shirt. I pushed the button on the wall next to the first-floor elevator. The door slid back immediately. I peered inside. Fifteen pairs of nun's eyes peered back. *How many fucking nuns can fit in one elevator!* It was like a convention in there. They must have been the advance party. I stared at the holy flock, then looked at my body awash with Budweiser. There was nothing else I could do but mumble my apology.

'Sorry, Sisters. . .'

One of the smiling group interrupted me as she cleared a space for me. She spoke on behalf of the congregation.

'. . . No need to apologise, son. No need at all. After all, wasn't our sacred Lord Jesus's first miracle the changing of the water into wine at the wedding feast of Cana?'

I was grateful. I joined her and her flock and endured the most uncomfortable elevator ride of my life. I nodded, they nodded. I smiled, they smiled. No more words were said. I was glad to get to the room to share my loot and my tale with Alan. He shared my bewilderment.

'Where the fuck did they come from, though?'

I raised my hands. I had no answer. I never saw another nun the whole time we remained in that empty hotel in the middle of nowhere. Where did they come from and where did they go? I have no idea. I suppose the Lord really does work in mysterious ways.

A familiar voice and a kind gesture

'Hello. Sorry to disturb you on a Friday night, but would it be possible to speak to Paul? It's John Motson here.'

He needn't have bothered providing his name. I recognised his voice from the first words he spoke down the telephone line. It was one of the most recognisable voices for any football fan, certainly of my generation. I asked him why he was calling me, and how he'd come by my number. Turned out he was calling me because he hoped that I, as Newcastle United's physiotherapist, could tell him discreetly who was likely to be fit and who was not likely to feature in our upcoming FA Cup fixture.

'So sorry for disturbing you on a Friday night, but I'm making last-minute preparations for my commentary on tomorrow's fixture and I like to be as fully prepared as possible. Please rest assured I won't share any information you can kindly provide me with.'

I didn't quite know how to respond. I didn't want to disappoint a national treasure, but I also had no intention of sharing any sensitive information regarding Newcastle United's possible team line-up with that national treasure.

Sensing my reticence, John Motson interrupted my silence.

'Alan Shearer gave me your number, but I can sense I've made you uncomfortable. Would it help if I hung up? Then maybe you can call Alan who will vouch for my integrity? We can speak after that if you are OK to do so? You have my number on your phone now. Just call back if you feel you want to. If you don't, then I fully understand and I won't trouble you again. Have a good evening.'

As polite and charming as he was, he was right. I was extremely uncomfortable about providing any sensitive information to him – or to anyone else for that matter. It wasn't something I'd ever done before or even contemplated doing before.

I hung up and called Alan. He informed me emphatically that I could trust John Motson to use any information I provided only for the purposes of aiding his diligent preparations for the game. I trusted Alan implicitly, and was therefore content with his endorsement of John's integrity.

I called him back. I gave him the information he required. He thanked me profusely. I spoke with John Motson for over an hour that night. He was a man I'd never met, but we talked about football, family and life in general. The following day after the game, I was in the treatment room, attached to the home dressing room at St James' Park. There was a knock on the door. As I opened it, John Motson, wrapped in his trademark sheepskin jacket, held out his hand to me. In it, were three PlayStation games.

'You mentioned on our call that your boys had a PlayStation. I hope they enjoy these ones. Thanks for all of the help you gave me.'

With that he was gone. It was a very kind gesture from an ultra-professional gentleman.

Ruining Bobby Robson's training session

End-of-season trips were usually very relaxed affairs. The gruelling season was complete and preseason preparations were still a long way over the horizon. It was a chance for players and staff alike to enjoy a bit of time together, usually in the lap of luxury in some far-flung exotic location. Ordinarily these were relaxed affairs, but not when Bobby Robson was the manager. When Newcastle United landed in Trinidad and Tobago, in the summer of 2000, Bobby Robson treated the jaunt like we were there to take part in the World Cup.

Bobby was a brilliant man, a dedicated man. He was determined to be professional at all times, and he demanded the same from everyone. I will never forget the look on the faces of players and staff alike when Bobby held a debrief on our arrival in Tobago. He informed the touring party there was to be no drinking alcohol, and there was a 10 p.m. curfew so we could all be refreshed for the first training session the following morning. I will also never forget how quickly we all scattered from the hotel bar at 10.15 p.m. when the great man strolled through the door to ensure we were adhering to his curfew. No one could question Bobby Robson's professionalism. I learned that the hard way the following day.

We had our first training session on a stiflingly hot day. After only 10 minutes of the session, the dehydrated players were gasping for a drink. They gathered around the water coolers. Bobby screamed at them.

'Don't drink the cold water! It'll give you tummy aches, you silly buggers!'

No one drank the cold water. The only problem was there was no warm water to drink instead. So no one drank anything. Bobby decided to complete his arduous session with a shooting exercise. As he set up his session, it dawned on him that he was short in numbers.

He was scratching his head and mumbling to himself as the thirsty players sheltered under a nearby tree to escape the punishing sun.

Bobby was about to abort his shooting session altogether before I volunteered to stand in and help him out. Obviously, I was a physiotherapist, but I had played professionally before for Newcastle United. I was more than capable of fulfilling the role required that day.

My job was a very simple one. All I had to do was to stand on the edge of the 18-yard box. Players would then drill the ball to my feet, and I'd lay it off for them to have a shot at goal. Bobby was grateful for my offer. I got into position on the dustbowl of a pitch. It was a dreadful surface – basically just sand with a few tufts of grass sticking up here and there. Robert Lee was first in line. I could see the devilment in his eyes, even before he drilled a pass ridiculously hard in my direction. The speeding ball collided with a tuft of grass about a metre in front of me. It shot off the tuft. I made a frantic attempt to anticipate where it was headed before it smacked me on the forehead and bounced over to where Bobby Robson was standing. He was shaking his head at me.

'Stop. Stop. Stop . . . ,' Bobby shouted, as he marched toward me shaking his finger in unison with his head. 'Son. Son. Son. If you can't play, you shouldn't be here. You're ruining the bloody session for the rest of us!'

I shook my head back at him.

'Jesus Christ, man. It hit a tuft of grass. Pelé couldn't have controlled that!'

The Newcastle United manager wasn't in the mood for my protestations. He wagged his finger and dismissed me from his session.

'Son. Pelé's mum could've controlled that! Get off!'

I trudged towards the group of Newcastle United footballers, now roaring with laughter at the sight of the former England and Barcelona manager dismissing his hapless physiotherapist from the training pitch for having a poor first touch. I'd nearly reached them when Bobby's conscience got the better of him. He called me back to my position at the edge of the box. I've never been so nervous in my life as I was that day, fending off balls right left and centre, while the perfectionist former England manager scrutinised every move I made. I didn't mis-control another pass – no matter how hard the ball was being driven at me. I was relieved when Bobby Robson blew his whistle to signal the session was complete and my torture was finally over. Bobby approached me.

'Much better, son. Much better.'

I grabbed a water bottle out of the cooler so I could have a much-needed drink after my job well done. Bobby knocked it out of my hand.

'Don't drink the cold water, it will give you tummy cramps, you silly bugger!'

He walked off shaking his head once more. I drank the water anyway. I figured a physio with stomach cramps wasn't going to derail Newcastle United's trip to Trinidad and Tobago. Neither was my poor first touch.

Not that my first touch was poor. Pelé with his mum's assistance couldn't have controlled that first deflected bullet! Try telling the ever-professional Bobby Robson that, though.

The day before the UEFA Cup semi-final v Marseille in May 2004. The game was played in the best atmosphere I ever experienced, anywhere in Europe.

'You've changed...'

Dr Richard Steadman, the world-renowned knee surgeon, holidayed in Paris in August 2001. I know that because along with Alan Shearer, I briefly disturbed his vacation. After two career-saving knee surgeries, and a very intense rehabilitation programme, Alan was finally ready to return to the fray. We just needed Dr Steadman's final sign-off. After three arduous trips to Colorado over the previous nine months, neither of us fancied another trip to the USA, especially for what was likely to be a 30-minute consultation. Dr Steadman kindly agreed to our request to interrupt his holiday in Paris instead. Newcastle United booked us into the George V Hotel, located just off the Champs-Élysées. We were barely through the front door before the very excited hotel manager accosted Alan Shearer.

'Mr Shearer, it is an honour to have you as our guest. Please accept my invitation for you and your colleague to share our penthouse suite for the duration of your stay.'

It was a grand gesture delivered with exuberant enthusiasm. We checked in and followed the flamboyant hotel manager towards the elevator. Alan nudged me and smiled.

'I've told you before, man. Stick with me. I'll look after you.'

He was right. Upgrades to first class on flights and now a penthouse suite in one of the grandest abodes in Paris. The perks of fame and fortune were mine for an all too brief period.

When we got to the suite, it was breathtaking. There were views across Paris from every window. An opulently furnished living room, fit for Marie Antionette, led into en-suite bedrooms on either side. Each bedroom was bigger than my entire family home in Newcastle. The bed was the size of my living room and the whirlpool bath could've fitted four people. Alan thanked the manager and turned to me.

'Not bad for two working-class lads, eh?'

I dropped my bag onto the chaise longue by the window that overlooked the Eiffel Tower. I was grateful to find myself surrounded by such opulence, but also conflicted. I was excited to be there but was aware of just how ridiculously decadent this world was compared to that of my childhood growing up on our council estate in Lisburn. I shared my thoughts.

'It's beautiful, no doubt about it. It's all a bit too posh for me if I'm honest. I don't really agree with such over-the-top luxury when half the world is starving. I would've been more comfortable in the standard room, or even in a less fancy hotel . . .'

Alan was having none of my guilt-filled nonsense.

'Oh fuck off, man! Just let your hair down for once, and enjoy yourself, you miserable bastard.'

I meant every word I'd said to him but I also knew he was right. I trudged reluctantly towards the giant double doors that led to my luxurious bedroom. We arranged to meet in two hours for dinner. Alan's words still rang in my ear as I shut the ornate doors behind me. I dropped my bags on the floor and headed for the en-suite to run a bath. Maybe Alan was right? Maybe I did need to relax a bit more. Just live in the moment. Bury my conscience. Forget about half the world starving . . .

Two and a half hours later, I felt a tap on my shoulder. It made me jump. I removed my headphones. Alan Shearer was standing over me. He was laughing and shaking his head.

'I thought you didn't like all this luxury and shit? Fuck me, man, it didn't take you too long to embrace it . . .'

Alan turned and walked out the door. He popped his head back around it and grinned.

'You've changed, man. You've changed.'

What caused such a reaction from Alan? That would be the sight confronting him when he entered my en-suite in search of me, because I was 30 minutes late for dinner. He'd found me lying in a whirlpool bath filled with bubbles. I wasn't alone either. I was in there with a complimentary bottle of champagne. Well, it would have been really silly of me not to drink it. After all, what else did I have to wash down my chocolate-dipped strawberries? That day, lying in that bubble bath, drunk on champagne, stuffed with chocolate-dipped strawberries while listening to Ennio Morricone through my earphones, is right up there with the most luxurious moments of my life. It may only be bettered by my first taste of a Curly Wurly in the early '70s, paid for with money I'd pinched from my mother.

Three days in the penthouse suite in the George V Hotel in Paris. Only a miserable bastard would turn his nose up at that, surely?

Besides, Alan did tell me to let my hair down and enjoy myself. I didn't want to disappoint him now, did I?

The Pied Piper of the Left Bank

We made our way along the Boulevard Saint-Michel. Alan Shearer was less than impressed by my impression of Peter Sarstedt's 'Where Do You Go To My Lovely'. I stopped singing only when we found the quaint bohemian hotel that housed Dr Richard Steadman and his family.

We sat in Dr Steadman's bedroom as I talked him through the rehabilitation programme Alan had completed with flying colours. It was a very relaxed conversation. We'd met the doctor on three occasions in Colorado, and also spoken to him every Friday morning throughout the weeks and months of the rehab period. It was like talking to an old friend, rather than the world's most eminent knee surgeon. After I'd finished talking through Alan's great progress, and Dr Steadman had examined Alan's knee, I was expecting the surgeon to give us the all-clear for Alan to return to full training. Dr Steadman, it seemed, had other plans.

'I'd like you to put Alan through a training drill. There's a park over the road. Let's have a session with plenty of twisting, turning, stopping, starting and jumping. Lots and lots of jumping.'

I was impressed with his diligence but told him we might have a slight problem.

'That would be fine, but we weren't expecting to train. I'm afraid Alan doesn't have any training kit with him. There'd be another slight issue if we were to train over there. Alan is one of the world's most famous footballers and the park over the road is bursting with families having picnics.'

Alan was nodding in agreement. Dr Steadman was less than impressed. And undeterred, he was already rummaging in his suitcase. Ten minutes later, the world's most expensive footballer was making his way towards a very busy public park dressed in a shirt and a pair of Dr Richard Steadman's khaki holiday shorts. It would be fair to say that Dr Steadman was a considerably larger man than Alan Shearer. So much so that Alan was forced to hold on to the bunched-up shorts to prevent them ending up around his ankles.

I accompanied the world-famous footballer, and the world's greatest knee surgeon, into the park. As a gentle introduction to our session, I instructed Alan to go for a slow jog around the perimeter. He'd barely taken 10 paces before the first excited child was shouting: 'Shearer, Shearer' and had begun to jog along behind him. I talked with Dr Steadman and we watched as more and more children joined the first one and ran after Alan. Chants of 'Shearer, Shearer' rang out around the park. Dr Steadman shook his head.

'I guess I underestimated how famous this guy is in Europe. He's like the Pied Piper of Paris.'

Alan and his entourage returned, his new fans spread out in a circle around us. I put Alan through his rehab routine to rapturous cheers, thunderous clapping and the occasional bursts of laughter when he struggled to keep a hold of Dr Steadman's shorts. The strangest training session I've ever been involved with, ended with Alan Shearer signing hundreds of autographs for excited and somewhat bewildered families in a picnic park on the Rive Gauche. More importantly, though, Dr Richard Steadman gave Alan the green light to return to full training. He also generously offered him the opportunity to keep the khaki shorts. The offer was politely declined.

A Man for All Seasons

Our trip to Paris, to consult with Dr Steadman, was organised by Tony Toward. Everything that happens at Newcastle United seems to be organised by Tony Toward. Tony Toward is very good at organising matters at Newcastle United. He should be, he has been organising things since 1979 and he's still organising them today. I met this quiet, diligent, kind man when I was a boy of 16 in 1981. Back then, he was one of three individuals who comprised the entire administration team of Newcastle United. Tony was the office junior; Ken Slater, the company accountant; and Russell Cushing, the company secretary. They worked out of a little suite of offices above the old ticket office, opposite the main stands. The club has changed beyond all recognition since those days, but one constant remains. Tony Toward is now in his 46th year at the club and currently Teams Operations Manager. He works intimately with the coaching and playing staff. He is ultra-professional, ultra-loyal, and incredibly well respected by colleagues past and present. Tony has given his life to Newcastle United – and the club is a better place for it.

Elevation

U2 played Earls Court, London, on 18 August, 2001. Newcastle United played at Chelsea at Stamford Bridge, London, on 19 August. I wasn't scheduled to be at either event until the morning of the U2 gig. I was meant to be rehabilitating Alan Shearer in Newcastle. Until, that is, my star patient breezed into the treatment room.

'Give Geraldine a ring and let her know you won't be home tonight.'

I was slightly puzzled.

'Why. Where are am I going?'

'Not just you. We. We're going to see that Irish band you're always banging on about. We can stay overnight in London so we can go to the Chelsea game as well. Don't worry about the cost. It's on me. Call it a thank for all your help in getting me fit.'

I was on the phone to Geraldine before he'd finished speaking. A few hours later I was on the train to London with Alan. We had a few drinks on the train, checked in to a great hotel, and had a few more drinks there too. Then we made our way to Earls Court and were escorted into the VIP lounge. The place was rammed. We barely got through the door before we were boxed into a corner as far away from the bar as it was possible to be.

This was real now, though. I was about to see my favourite live band once more. I could feel my heart thumping against my chest wall with the giddy excitement of it all or maybe because of the alcohol on the train and in the hotel. I could hardly hear Alan as he shouted over the noise. I worked out he was asking me what I wanted to drink.

I had offered to buy him one as a thank you, but he was determined I wasn't to spend a penny. He pushed his way through the crowd. I could see him bobbing and weaving, but he wasn't moving anywhere. He was struggling to get anywhere near the bar. Then suddenly my ears were filled with an almighty roar coming from the arena next door. It signalled only one thing: U2 were on stage. My head was buzzing, my heart jumping and my feet getting ready to run. I shouted to the back of Alan's bobbing head. I screamed at him. I told him to leave the drinks. He didn't hear me, he was on manoeuvres. I tried to get near him, I couldn't. A drunken wave was pushing me in the opposite direction towards the door. The crowd in the arena next door erupted once more. I could hear the genius of the Edge's guitar, Adam's pulsing bass, Larry hammering the drums, then Bono, fucking Bono, starting his beautiful wail of an intro to the opening song, 'Elevation'.

'Yeah, Yeah . . . Woo Hoo . . . Woo Hoo . . .'

I thought my heart was going to explode. In that moment, it was all too much. I forgot all about Alan's struggles to reach the VIP bar. I just turned and ran with the crowd. I ran as fast I could straight to the brilliant seats in the front row Alan had secured for us. I got there just as the house lights dropped and U2 burst into a ball of raging energy. It was the most exhilarating moment I've ever experienced at a live gig. Almost spiritual. I was still in a trance halfway through the second song of the set, 'Beautiful Day', when Alan made his way towards me carrying two pints of lager in plastic cups. I had forgotten all about him until that moment. He shook his head and handed me a pint as he spoke.

'Let me get this straight. I paid for your first-class train ticket. I paid for your hotel. I paid for your ticket to the gig and I got you into the VIP lounge, then you just fucked off and left me there!'

I felt a sudden twinge of guilt. He was right. I raised my plastic cup and my shoulders. 'Thank you. Sorry man, but it's U2. It's U fucking 2.'

I don't think I spoke another word to Alan that night. I was too mesmerised by what was within touching distance of me on the stage in front of us. It may well have been the best U2 gig I've ever seen. It was unquestionably the best opening. And I have seen many! I know I would never have been there without the kind gesture of a great man. I wasn't even sure if Alan Shearer liked U2, or if he enjoyed the gig. That is until not long afterwards, when his daughter posted a video of him driving through Newcastle. Alan was listening to U2 and belting out 'Elevation' at the top of his lungs. It's a shame he didn't actually get to see them sing it that night at Earls Court. He was too busy trying to get to the bar. I can say it was unforgettable. I can also say I was extremely grateful to him for getting me there. Even if it didn't quite appear that way on the night.

Alan Shearer or Elliot Lee?

I have many happy memories of family parties at Rob Lee's welcoming home in Durham. There were a group of us who always gathered there. It was the best friendship group I experienced in my almost two-decade career at the club, and included Alan Shearer, Gary Speed, Shay Given, Steve Harper and Rob Lee from the playing staff. Then there was Derek Wright, Ray Thompson, Dr Roddy Macdonald, the club surgeon Rob Gregory, and me. Rob and his wife Anna were generous hosts. They provided great food, and plenty of alcohol. They were magical days. I looked forward to my regular invitations.

One sunny afternoon in late August 2001 stands out way above the others in my memory. After a BBQ, someone suggested an impromptu football match. All the kids were involved, all of the international footballers were involved, and all of the staff were involved too. My eldest son, Conor, was nine at the time. He and Olly Lee, Rob's eldest, were designated as team captains, and their job was to pick the teams. After much deliberation, and some very unusual player picks, Conor was left with the last two players to choose from. It was a straight choice between the former England captain and world's most expensive footballer, Alan Shearer, or Rob's youngest son, seven-year-old Elliot Lee. An easy decision for Conor; he didn't even hesitate.

'I choose Elliot!'

The look of faux rejection on Alan's face was surpassed only by the look of genuine joy on seven-year-old Elliot Lee's.

It will be no surprise that my eldest son never ever did become a football manager. Elliot Lee, however, did go on to become a professional footballer in his own right. Maybe nine-year-old Conor saw something we didn't. In Conor's defence Alan was coming back from injury at the time and not at peak fitness. Mind you, he did still manage to score most of the goals that day.

Bono's glasses

I was on my family vacation in June 2002, and awoke to six voicemails. The first four were from Gary Speed. They'd been left in the early hours of the morning. There was music blaring in the background.

'Pick up the phone.'

'Pick up the phone.'

'Answer your phone.'

'Answer your fucking phone!'

They were followed by two from Alan Shearer.

'Pick up your phone, man!'

'We're with Bono. Pick up your fucking phone!'

Both men were acutely aware of my borderline obsession with U2. They'd thought it would be a lovely idea to get the great man on the phone to speak with me. It certainly would have been!

Three weeks later, I met with Alan for a workout and a coffee at a local leisure facility. He was waxing lyrical about bumping into Bono and the Edge, in a nightclub in Dublin. He said they'd spent some time with them and he was amazed at just how down to earth, warm and friendly they were. I told him I wasn't too bothered at all about meeting my idols from U2 or talking to them on the phone.

'The whole celebrity hero worship stuff leaves me cold. I just love their music. That's good enough for me.'

Alan was less than convinced. He put his hand inside his jacket pocket, and then threw the contents across the table.

'You won't be wanting those, then. I got them for you.'

I stared at his gift. It was a pair of Bono's glasses. Bono's fucking glasses! Not just any pair either, but the iconic wraparound Bulgari glasses he wore on stage. I picked them up to study them.

'Both lenses are signed, one by Bono, the other by the Edge.'

I tried to play it cool. I didn't want to come across like the excited teenager I was inside. I sat them down and pushed them across the table. I reiterated my earlier point.

'You keep them. I'm not into all that celebrity worship stuff. You should know that by now, man.'

Alan shook his head and pushed Bono's glasses back in my direction.

'Just take the glasses, man. You know you want them.'

I shrugged my shoulders and casually slipped them into my jacket pocket.

'Ok. But only 'cos you've insisted. Thank you.'

I was ridiculously excited as we were leaving the car park. Alan drove to the security barrier. I followed. I pulled to a stop behind his car. My phone rang. I picked it up. It was Alan.

'Take the fucking glasses off, you sad bastard. I can see you in my mirror!'

I'd only put them on for a second. Honestly! I'm not into all that celebrity hero worship stuff. OK. Maybe with one exception.

It would be fair to say that wasn't the last time the glasses have made an appearance. I wore them as part of a fancy dress outfit on New Year's Eve in my village pub. A drunk middle-aged woman approached me in a frenzy. She was convinced I was Bono. I think the bottle and a half of Prosecco swirling around her brain may have contributed to her levels of certainty. She wasn't having anybody tell her I wasn't actually Bono. I tried to convince her.

'D'you really think the multimillionaire front man of one of the biggest rock bands in the world is likely to be spending his New Year's Eve at a fancy dress party in The Lion and Lamb in Horsley, Northumberland?'

She still wasn't having it.

'You could be. You might have family here for all I know.'

She swigged her Prosecco. I tried again.

'OK. Just say I am Bono and I have family here . . .'

'I knew it. I fucking knew it . . .'

'Whoa, woah. I'm not Bono! I'm pointing out that if I was Bono and I did happen to find myself in Horsley village on New Year's Eve and there just so happened to be a fancy dress party in the village pub, it is extremely unlikely that I'd choose to come dressed as Bono. I'm more likely to come as John Lennon, or a Teletubby, or anyone else other than Bono surely.'

That seemed to do the trick for her. She staggered off and I was Bono no more. I was glad I'd finally convinced her I wasn't. I was also a little sad. In truth, I think I enjoyed being Bono a tad too much that night for however short a period it lasted.

Footballing icon is often a term that is overused. Not in this instance. A man of incredible substance.

The King of Barcelona

In December 2002, Newcastle United's Champions League game with Barcelona was postponed for a day. That gave recently knighted Sir Bobby Robson a rare opportunity to take his backroom staff out for a stroll and a quiet drink in one of the many bars surrounding our team hotel. I'm not sure what our modest manager was expecting in terms of a reaction from the people of Barcelona, but I really don't think he expected the response he got. We were barely out of the front door of our hotel before the first gentleman asked Bobby for his autograph. Then someone else asked for a photo. Then a car horn honked as the passengers waved to our manager. We walked around the harbour. A restauranteur opened his door and asked Bobby to come inside. The rest of us sheepishly followed. I'm glad we did. One by one, each table stood to applaud the very proud, and visibly moved, Newcastle United manager. We hung around the reception area while Bobby visited every table, signing autographs and posing for photographs. When he finally came back to us, he was very obviously bursting with pride.

'Did you see that, boys? Did you see that? Wasn't it marvellous? Wasn't it bloody marvellous!'

He turned towards the room and waved to his adoring subjects. They clapped and cheered him. The boy from Langley Park was the King of Barcelona that night. It meant the world to him. And witnessing it was a beautiful experience.

We finally made it to a pub. We were about to go in when Newcastle United Director Douglas Hall exited and walked towards our group.

'I wouldn't go in there, lads. It's very rowdy.' As he and his entourage made their way past us, our grinning Knight of the Realm, and recently crowned King of Barcelona, waved us towards the entrance.

'Come on, boys. We'll be safe enough.'

The pub was full of Newcastle United fans. It erupted with chants of 'There's only one Bobby Robson . . .'

I couldn't agree more. Bobby beamed with pride. A great manager and an outstanding man. The good people of Barcelona and Newcastle certainly agreed on both counts that memorable night.

A dedicated superstar

Newcastle was blanketed in snow on 22 February, 2004. I know that for certain because we were forced to switch my son Owen's seventh birthday party from its original venue. Luckily, we were able to use Newcastle United's indoor pitch and the training ground canteen as an alternative last-minute venue.

Changing the venue was the easy part. Such was the deluge that it still proved one hell of a slog to get there on a Sunday morning. Many roads were closed, the city was deserted. It was one of those days when the advice from the Met Office is to stay indoors unless travel is absolutely necessary. The north-east was a whiteout. When we few hardy souls arrived at the training ground in Longbenton, we were very surprised to find that the indoor hangar was already open and the lights were on. I prised open the frozen door and guided the boys and their parents into the cold cavernous space. Then we stood and watched as an instantly recognisable lone figure practised his kicking drills at the far end of the hangar.

It had been three months since England won the Rugby World Cup. Half of the boys in our group had been so inspired by that triumph that they were wearing England Rugby tops emblazoned with 'Jonny Wilkinson'. Now those same boys stood dumbstruck as that very same Jonny Wilkinson stopped what he was doing and made his way smiling towards us. When he reached us, he spent 30 minutes chatting to the boys and their equally starstruck parents. The boys played football for an hour on one side of the hangar while Jonny Wilkinson did a fine impression of a metronome at the other. He was still kicking balls when we left. I drove home in complete awe of his dedication to his craft.

When the snow had come and other sportsman were postponing their sessions, Jonny Wilkinson had sought out the only available place in an entire city just so that he could continue to perfect his art. He did that *after* he'd already scored the drop goal that won the World Cup. Incredible.

An iconic celebration

In my latter years as a physiotherapist at Newcastle United, I had a treatment room at my home. My intention was to create a thriving private practice away from the club. I wanted to leave behind the demands of professional football eventually and enjoy a better quality of life with my young family. In truth the treatment room was a white elephant. I was often too busy at the club or too tired when I came home to even contemplate an evening treating private patients. I said no to most requests I received.

Alan Shearer was an exception. He would come over for treatment on occasion, usually on the off season. He did so in the early summer of 2004. My youngest son Ciaran was three years old at the time. Alan was lying on the treatment table when Ciaran entered the room proudly wearing his Newcastle United strip. Despite the full strip, my talkative three-year-old was completely oblivious to the fact that he was in the presence of the great Alan Shearer himself. Alan struck up a conversation with him.

'What team do you support?'

'Newcastle.'

'Who's your favourite player.'

Ciaran turned to show him *Shearer* across his back as he answered.

'Alan Shearer.'

'Why do you like him?'
'Because he's the best player.'
'Is he?'
'Yeah. And he's my daddy's friend. My daddy works for Newcastle, you know.'

Alan was enjoying himself.

'Alan Shearer is your daddy's friend, is he? And what does your daddy do?'
'He's a physio. He makes Alan better.'
'And what does Alan do when he's better?'
'He scores the goals.'

Alan had one more question.

'What does Alan do when he scores the goals?'

Ciaran didn't answer. Instead he raised his three-year-old arm to the sky, and ran around and around Alan Shearer until his mum came and dragged him out of the room. The innocence of it all still brings a smile to my face all these years later.

Forever linked to another United, but Nicky Butt also gave his all when at Newcastle United. A hugely impressive character off the pitch too.

The humble winner

When Nicky Butt joined Newcastle United in 2004, he did so as an eight-time Premier League winner, three-time FA Cup winner and a Champion's League winner. He was certainly the most decorated footballer I encountered in all my 18 years at the club. He had been an integral part of Sir Alex Ferguson's all-conquering Manchester United team of the last decade. He was a fully paid-up member of the fabled Class of '92, alongside Ryan Giggs, David Beckham, Paul Scholes and the Neville brothers. Nicky Butt was footballing royalty. He was also the most humble, down-to-earth footballer I ever encountered. From the day he walked through the door, until the day he left, he gave the very best of himself, often in difficult circumstances.

I instantly warmed to him as a person. And I was very glad he was still at the club when I returned as part of Alan Shearer's management team at the end of the disastrous 2008/09 season. In our short time there, when it was abundantly clear that others had downed tools, Nicky Butt remained committed to the cause. He'd initially intended to retire that summer. However, after our relegation, he signed a new one-year contract. He felt, that as one of the players responsible for the relegation, he had a duty to stay and try to make things right. The following summer, he lifted the championship trophy as club captain, completing the job he had set out to do.

What an impressive man.

'It's only a bit of bloody wind...'

Sir Bobby Robson was obsessed with football. On reflection, I think he was more than obsessed. He was consumed by it. When the Twin Towers were attacked on 11 September, 2001, I was sitting in a hospitality lounge at St James' Park in Newcastle. We'd just finished our lunch. Bobby Robson stood up and readied himself to turn off the TV so that he could update the group on preparations for the upcoming fixture. He'd only just risen to his feet when the first plane hit. He paused for a moment while everyone in the room stared in disbelief. As we watched the smoke billowing from the building where the plane had entered, another plane crashed into the second tower. I think that was the moment when everyone in the room realised the enormity of what had occurred. This was no tragic accident.

A frantic murmur swept across the room, as players and staff offered theories and counter-theories as to what the world was witnessing. Nothing else mattered except the horror unfolding in front of our eyes. Everyone in the room was focused solely on the TV screen. Everyone, that is, except Bobby Robson. His focus was on football and nothing was going to distract him. He watched as the second plane hit. He shook his head, clearly concerned at what was unfolding, then shouted to one of the coaches who was holding the TV remote, signalling to him simultaneously.

'It's a tragedy. Give it the gun.'

The coach obligingly turned off the TV, and Bobby began talking about the subject that consumed him. While he set out the arrangements for the following few days, I slipped out of the room, ran downstairs and phoned Geraldine to ask if she was watching the drama unfolding. Of course she was. The whole world was. The whole world apart from the players of Newcastle United. They were upstairs listening to their football-obsessed manager discussing the team shape for the upcoming fixture. There was nothing heartless in Bobby Robson's behaviour. I simply believe he was so focused on football, he was incapable of fully comprehending the horror.

If Bobby was consumed by football, he was also a perfectionist. If he had a point to make, or something to impart to his players in a training session, nothing, or no one, would prevent him from doing so. That personality trait was never more evident than on Newcastle United's summer tour to Hong Kong in 2004. We stayed in the luxurious Harbour Grand Hotel. The wall-to-ceiling windows in our bedrooms afforded us spectacular views of Kowloon across the harbour. All was going to plan until we were informed by the authorities that we were expected to be hit by a typhoon at some point the following day.

We were told that we were to stay in the bathroom of our bedrooms for the duration of the storm, because the previous typhoon had blown 80 of the hotel bedroom windows into the rooms. For all of us, that was more than a little unnerving. The following day's scheduled training session would be postponed while we bunkered down in our bathrooms. At least, that's what should have happened. Sir Bobby Robson was having none of it. He spoke with the authorities.

The plans changed. We were now permitted to train the following morning, with the proviso that we were safely back in the hotel and in our bathrooms by lunchtime. The typhoon was due to rip through the harbour in the early afternoon.

A bunch of nervous players and staff took part in the morning session. It was all a bit of a farce as the wind was already howling when we got to the training facility. Someone would strike a ball in one direction and the wind would carry it off into the trees in the other. Everyone couldn't wait for it to be over, so that we could get back to the safety of our bedroom toilets. We were a relieved group as we made our way towards the coach at the designated time. We all boarded, apart from Sir Bobby, two young strikers and a goalkeeper. On the coach, there were concerned questions as to what could possibly be delaying the manager. Then it became apparent that he was still on the training pitch, perfecting some shooting drills. The bus was rocking from side to side. The howling wind whipping up one hell of a storm. The frightened players were getting more than a little anxious. I climbed off the coach with John Carver. We battled winds that threatened to blow us off our feet. We called out to Sir Bobby to remind him of the time. He took some persuading to abort his drill, oblivious to the possible consequences of the time delay. And totally lost in the moment of his coaching.

We held on to each other as we fought our way back to the bus. The vehicle rocked and swayed its way through empty streets, as the gathering storm raged all around us. The rocking bus finally reached the hotel. I paused to let Sir Bobby Robson leave his seat. I told him I was grateful to be back. He shook his head and smiled.

'I don't know what the world is coming to, son. Cutting training sessions short. It's only a bit of bloody wind, after all!'

I smiled as I replied.

'That's certainly one way of describing a typhoon, I suppose.'

Sir Bobby simply had no idea of the danger he was in. His focus was on football. Only football. Nothing was more important to him than that. Certainly not a bit of bloody wind.

'What's my name?'

Dutch superstar Patrick Kluivert joined Newcastle United in July 2004. It was always interesting when such a high profile individual arrived at the club. *How will he gel with the group? How well will he interact with the staff? How big will his ego be?* More often than not, the more high profile the individual, the more down to earth he tended to be. Patrick Kluivert was no exception. He was a joy to work with from the moment Sir Bobby Robson proudly brought him into the treatment room and introduced him. Even if he did seem to have a problem remembering my name for the remainder of his short spell at Newcastle United.

The staff wore training kit with our initials on. On that first day when I shook Patrick Kluivert's hand he smiled, studied the initials *PF* on my training top and said, 'It's lovely to meet you, Phil.'

I naturally corrected him and told him that my name was in fact Paul, and not Phil. Patrick smiled again, apologised profusely, then proceeded to call me Phil for the rest of his time at the club!

Towards the end of his short spell at Newcastle United, Patrick picked up an injury and spent some time in rehab with me. I was in the treatment room with him and Alan Shearer. Patrick was enjoying a laugh with Alan and 'Phil'. Alan spoke to me, 'Hey, Phil. Why don't you take Patrick out and play him a game of two touch?'

Patrick laughed at the suggestion that chubby 'Phil' could possibly compete with him. After all, he was one of the greatest strikers of his generation and certainly one of the most technically gifted. I seized my moment.

'I tell you what, Patrick, if I beat you, then from this day onwards my name's Paul. No more Phil. What d'you say?'

He was already laughing his way towards the door.

'Sure. That works for me. Let's see what you've got, Phil.'

I smiled back at Patrick as he held the door for me.

'You know this won't be as easy as you think, don't you?'

He patted my head.

'Oh don't worry, Phil. I'm sure I'll be fine.'

When you're a physiotherapist at a professional football club, you tend to spend a ridiculous amount of time with a ball at your feet. When you were also once a professional footballer, back in the dark distant past, and you now spend every day playing two touch, you really do tend to get remarkably good. Even a superstar footballer will be somewhat at a disadvantage, especially if he doesn't regularly play 'two touch'. A supposedly inferior opponent – i.e. an overweight physiotherapist – but one who has been playing two touch every day for 10 years or more, might just cause an upset.

When we got back to the treatment room, Alan Shearer was still there. He asked who'd won. I cupped my ear as I spoke to Patrick.

'What's my name, Patrick?'

The great man shook his head and laughed, before he replied rather sheepishly.

'Your name is Paul.'

I cupped my ear once more.

'What's that? I didn't hear you?'

He slapped me on the back.

'I said your name is Paul, and you're a fucking bandit, my friend.'

Patrick spoke to Alan.

'His touch is fucking good, man.'

I basked in my glory.

The following morning, Patrick Kluivert opened the treatment room door.

I greeted him as he approached me.

'Morning, Patrick.'

He flashed me a smile and shook my hand,

'Morning, Phil.'

Some battles you just can't win. But the two touch . . . that, I did win.

Patrick Kluivert and Nicky Butt in 2004. Two players I would have loved to have seen at St James' Park earlier in their careers.

One player, two managers

Craig Bellamy was one of my favourite players to watch at Newcastle United. He was a raging ball of energy. He had great pace, aggression and awareness, and was a very intelligent footballer. He was a potent weapon for any team he played for, and a genuine threat to any team he played against. But he also proved to be a difficult character to manage for all those who undertook that onerous task. I witnessed first-hand two experienced managers take very different approaches to managing Craig Bellamy. Both managers were forced to grapple with what were essentially the same set of circumstances. How they chose to deal with the problem facing them was telling, and their respective approaches led to entirely different outcomes.

In October 2004, the Sky TV match-day cameras allegedly caught Craig Bellamy mouthing off in the direction of then manager Graeme Souness. Craig was simply a spiky individual. Anyone who worked with him would testify to that. I suspect Craig Bellamy himself would concur.

Two days after the Sky TV broadcast incident, Graeme Souness called a team meeting. He wanted to discuss some issues that had arisen over recent days. The manager had a ferocious reputation back in his prime as a player. As he began to talk, he did so in a calm and collected manner befitting his advancing years, health issues and no little experience as a manager. Talking through the various incidents that had unfolded over recent days, he made it clear that he wasn't happy with the behaviour of certain players. His words were listened to with quiet respect. Graeme Souness was still a picture of controlled authority as he turned his attention to Craig. Then everything changed. The manager had barely begun to speak before Craig began muttering at him and shaking his head. There would be no quiet respect coming from Craig Bellamy. The muttering and head-shaking flicked a switch in Graeme. All calm, all control just vanished. In their place was anger and aggression.

The manager reeled off the trophies he'd won and the clubs he'd played for and then challenged Craig directly over the alleged comments he'd made on camera.

He made a grab for him.

'In the gym now. Let's sort this out like fucking men!'

The room was momentarily stunned into silence and inertia before Alan Shearer and one or two of the other senior players pulled the enraged manager away from Craig. The incident was over as quickly as it had begun, but their relationship couldn't be salvaged. Bellamy may very well have been one of our best players, but within months he'd departed Newcastle United for good and the club lost one of its most valuable on-field assets.

Two years earlier, Sir Bobby Robson had entered the same players' lounge. There was no team meeting that day, just an obviously very angry manager. Bobby looked up at the TV monitor, where Craig Bellamy could clearly be seen mouthing obscenities in his direction during the weekend's fixture. Bobby was livid. He was making sure everyone in the room knew just how livid. He jabbed his finger towards the TV.

'Did you see that? Did you see that little bugger, swearing at me? I'm not having that. I'll sort him out. You mark my words . . .'

Bobby Robson was still in full angry flow when the door behind him opened. Craig Bellamy walked in. Bobby spun around. Everyone in the room held their collective breath for the moment when the enraged manager would surely give Craig a stern telling-off. Then nothing happened. Nothing at all. Bobby smiled. He put his arm around Craig Bellamy's shoulder.

'Morning, son. How's the hamstring? Not too bad, I hope. We need you for the weekend. Can't win without you. You'll make the difference.'

Bobby still had his arm around Craig as he winked and grinned to his audience in the room. It was quite the performance. It was brilliant. Bobby deserved a round of applause. Craig Bellamy did play that weekend. He played every weekend after that too. Outstandingly so.

Time for everyone in the stadium to have a chat, while some of us have to work!

During the remainder of Sir Bobby Robson's memorable tenure at Newcastle United, Craig often proved to be the difference between us winning and losing.

I don't know how I'd have reacted, or managed Craig Bellamy. He was the most difficult of difficult characters. How Graeme Souness chose to react is how I suspect most mere mortals would. I think most people would just move the difficult character along, and pass the problem over to another manager at another club. How Bobby Robson chose to deal with it? Well, that's why he is rightly remembered and revered as one of the greats. He tolerated the nonsense and got the best he could out of his prized asset, Craig Bellamy.

Two experienced managers, one difficult player. Different strategies produced wildly different results.

A date with a masseur

One of the many perks of my job as a physiotherapist at Newcastle United was a company car. Better than that, my car was changed every six months for a new model. On my changeover day in early 2005, a young girl from the car garage drove my new car to the training ground. I had a very brief conversation with her at the side of the training pitch, and she swapped my vehicle for a new one. That was the first and last time I ever met her. After training, one of the senior players approached me. I won't name him here to spare his blushes. He was someone who fancied himself as a bit of a ladies' man despite his marital status.

'D'you know that girl you were talking to? Could you get me her mobile number?'

I had a split second to decide: simply tell Romeo that I didn't know her and I couldn't get her number, or lie to him and create a little mischief. I chose the latter.

'Who, Jenny? Yeah, she's a good friend of mine. Just split from her husband. Great girl. She loves the football. Mad Newcastle fan too. Her number's in my phone. I'll get you it when we go back in. She'll be very excited if you call her, I'm sure.'

I called a friend and asked if his wife would be happy to play along with a prank. He put her on the phone. She was more than happy to help. The player came straight into the treatment room as soon as his training session was complete. He beamed as I handed him my friend's wife's phone number. I told him I'd spoken to Jenny and she was looking forward to his call.

She didn't have long to wait. He called her as he was leaving the treatment room. He gave me a thumbs up as Jenny greeted him warmly on the phone. Thinking he was making a date with the young girl from that morning, he arranged a time and place for their rendezvous. My friend's wife called me straight after to tell me the arrangements.

'He wants to meet at four this afternoon at your training ground. He says there will be no one around at that time, and we can have the place ourselves. Jesus, he's the last of the romantics, alright. A date at a training ground. He could at least take a girl out for a drink or something. Oh, and he told me to wear something sexy. I mean who the fuck tells someone to wear something sexy?'

'A randy, out of control footballer maybe?'

I thanked her for her help. I needed to put the remainder of the plan in place. I didn't have much time as our lothario was wasting none of his. I had a chat with the rest of the backroom staff. Within minutes we had our plan in place for when our unsuspecting player turned up for his date that afternoon.

As 4 p.m. approached, the usually bustling training complex was eerily quiet. Darkness was descending and the plush reception area was dimly lit and deserted. It was deserted apart from the presence of the entire non-playing staff of Newcastle United, including the manager, hiding in various rooms off the main thoroughfare. Romeo arrived right on time. His expensive aftershave wafted through the double doors alongside him. He was dressed in his finest and took a seat facing the doors he'd just passed through. His anticipation was palpable as he waited for Jenny to appear in her sexy clothes as instructed . . . and appear she did.

We had a great view of his face as he turned to follow the sound of Jenny's high heels clicking and clacking along the dark corridor behind him. We had an even better view of Jenny as she entered the reception area in all her finest. I will never forget the look in Romeo's eyes when he first set them upon the vision standing in front of him. Our masseur, all 6 foot 4 of him, appeared dressed in full drag, teetering on six-inch heels with two balloons stuffed into his silk blouse. It remains one of my favourite moments of all my time in football.

Our resident lothario stood open-mouthed for a second before slumping onto the chair behind him and burying his head in his hands. The howling laughter from the 15 members of the backroom staff who swirled around him could no doubt be heard from the main road a quarter of a mile away. Once he'd got over his embarrassment, he turned to me and smiled.

'You wanker.'

I shook his hand and laughed with him.

'Absolutely.'

40

My fortieth birthday celebrations in Dublin made for one of the most enjoyable and most memorable weekends of my life. Courtesy of Shay Given, we were able to obtain 20 tickets to see U2 at Croke Park in the summer of 2005. A group of close friends and family, including Alan Shearer and Rob Lee, enjoyed two magical days in my favourite city. Included in our allocation were six VIP tickets. There was a debate within the group as to who would be having the upgraded tickets. Well, when I say debate, I mean Alan Shearer, Rob Lee and their wives got four. The debate was around who would be allocated the other two. Wanting very much to be a man of the people, I stayed quiet while the others deliberated. Wanting very much to have the upgraded tickets, I was delighted when they came to the sensible conclusion that Geraldine and I could have them as it was after all my fortieth birthday. I 'reluctantly' accepted the will of the people and two hours later made my way towards Croke Park with Alan and Rob. We parted from the others in our group as they headed off to the cheap seats.

I was really looking forward to my VIP experience as we made our way into the main stand. We climbed the first set of stairs, then the next, then another one as we ascended all the way to the back of the giant stand. When we reached our seats in the gods I looked towards the stage where U2 would be performing as ants tonight.

40

My phone buzzed. It was Derek Wright calling me from the cheap seats. I followed his instructions until my eyes met the waving hands of the 14 others in our group. If they'd been any closer to the stage Bono would have had to ask them to move back a bit! This VIP experience was not living up to my expectations. I was about to say just that to Alan Shearer, but he was too busy coughing his lungs out because the man next to him just lit up the biggest joint I'd ever seen. Between coughing fits Alan was waving his arms and engaging in a heated conversation with the man.

'No smoking, mate. The sign says no smoking . . .'

He was wasting his breath. It clearly wasn't the first spliff his neighbour had sucked on that day. The more Alan complained, the more smoke the stoned bloke blew in our direction. Alan gave up in the end apart from head-shaking and waving his arms about until U2 came on stage. The band blasted out a rip-roaring version of 'Vertigo' to kick off what I hoped would be another exhilarating concert. The song finished, the crowd erupted, then I felt someone tugging on my shirt sleeve. I turned, only to be greeted by a rather worse for wear Rob Lee shaking his head at me. He spoke in his very distinctive, but slurred, cockney accent.

'What's this all about?'

I looked into his eyes for signs of life. There was still a flicker.

'What do you mean?'

He swayed and pointed in the general direction of the ants on the stage.

'This. That. Them. All of this shit. What's it all about?'

I looked in his eyes again. All intelligent life had departed for the night. I spun him around in the direction of the stage. After each and every song finished, he turned around and asked the same question. I spun him around until the next song ended. We repeated that dance right up until the opening bars of 'Where the Streets Have No Name' filled the Dublin sky. I lost my patience.

'Fuckin' hell, man. Rob, just watch the crowd and watch them enjoying themselves. That's what this is all about.'

He stared off somewhere into the distance as the whole stadium erupted. I'm still not quite sure he ever worked out what it was all about, but he never turned around again.

After the brilliant if somewhat stressful concert, we made our way to Lillie's Bordello in the city centre. Alan Shearer's presence ensured we were invited into the VIP lounge. Our old manager, Kevin Keegan, was in there alongside former England footballer Mick Channon. Kevin was his usual ebullient self. He wished me a happy birthday and offered to introduce me to Mick. I reminded him that I had in fact played with Mick Channon when he'd had a brief spell at Newcastle United in 1982. Kevin was very excited by that. He raced me over to Mick and introduced me.

'Mick. Mick. This is Paul Ferris. You won't remember him, but he used to play with you.' Not the best introduction I've ever had, Kevin!

The following day, more by osmosis than plan, we all ended up in O'Donoghue's Pub in Merrion Row, famous for its association with The Dubliners and later The Fureys. The Guinness flowed, and the locals in the corner playing the traditional music session were incredible. They were brilliant, mainly because there were several award-winning musicians in their number. Fuelled by the Guinness, encouraged my friends and family, and caught up in the occasion, I burst into a verse or two of my favourite song, 'Dirty Old Town'. I was loving the moment and belted out the song. I remembered every word too. I've never felt so Irish.

The cheers from my friends and family, and the effects of the Guinness I'd consumed convinced me I was killing it. Then I made the mistake of glancing at the poor musicians who were desperately trying to work out what key I was warbling in so they could accompany me, or maybe drown me out. I caught the eye of the old man in the middle playing his fiddle. He stopped when ours eyes met. He put his bow down and lowered his fiddle. Then slowly he began shaking his head from side to side. His lips were moving. I strained to read them. I wish I hadn't. They weren't that difficult to read actually. Just in case I missed it the first time he kindly repeated his words twice more for me.

'Fucking tourists . . .'

I got it the first time. I was killing it alright! Thankfully, and luckily for me, everyone in my party was too drunk to notice. I got to sing 'Dirty Old Town' in the same pub where Luke Kelly and Finbar Furey must have sung it too. Even if I'm just one of the many tourists who've done so over the years, I'll settle for that. I could have stayed in O'Donoghue's for the rest of that weekend. In fact, all of our group could have. The music was amazing, the Guinness was great and the atmosphere was magical. It was just one of those days when everything falls into place and all is well in the world.

We had a vote and the group decided to stay in the pub rather than go to the out-of-town restaurant we had booked for our evening meal. We were all set to stay until the one killjoy in the group shouted long and hard about why we needed to stick to our original plan. Alan Shearer can be very persuasive when he sets his mind to it. One by one he convinced us that, despite the fun we were having, it was unacceptable to cancel a booking for 20 people just hours before we were due to dine. We reluctantly agreed and our time in O'Donoghue's came to an abrupt end.

We arrived in Dalkey, the high spirits of the afternoon fading behind us. I pushed open the door to the plush establishment. It was completely deserted apart from five staff members, who greeted us enthusiastically at the door. A band in the far corner began playing as soon as we entered. The room was decorated beautifully and adorned with birthday banners and balloons. The manager greeted Alan Shearer like an old friend. Alan brought him to me. He shook my hand.

'Happy fortieth birthday, Mr Ferris. Mr Shearer has booked the entire restaurant for the evening. He will be taking care of all of the food and drink. A good friend to have, I would suggest.'

He'd booked the band too. A good friend indeed. It was a fitting finale to complete the best weekend of my life. That trip to Dublin, in the summer of 2005, is the one and only time in my life where I've booked a hotel and never slept in my room for the entirety of my stay. Wouldn't it be great if life was like that all the time?

I never have been heard singing in public since that memorable day in O'Donoghue's. Well, not when I'm sober anyway.

The Master Chronicler

The Chronicle (formerly *The Evening Chronicle*), a newspaper launched in 1885, is an institution as synonymous with the city of Newcastle as coal mining, ship building and the famous football team itself. When I arrived in the city in 1981 I used to wander past endless newspaper sellers in the city centre and marvel at how many imaginative ways they would find to shout the word *Chronicle* into the early evening air. Some of my favourites were *Crin-e-gil*, *Chronigaaaaal* and the always effective *Rrruunn-e-gal*.

Regardless of how it was pronounced, *The Evening Chronicle*, back in the '80s, was the oracle for anyone wanting to find out the latest goings on at Newcastle United. In many ways, and even with the advent of social media and instant digital reporting, it still is. To Newcastle United fans of a certain vintage, the sports pages of the *Chronicle* remain their go-to place for accurate stories on their local team. I've been reading the back pages of the *Chronicle* for over 40 years now. While the quality of the journalism has risen and fallen several times over that period, one man's work has stood head and shoulders above all others during that time. Sports editor John Gibson was first employed at *The Chronicle* in the mid '60s. It must have been a dream job for a Newcastle United-mad boy from Benwell, in the city's West End. I can't comment on his early work, but I've read a lot of his writing since 1981. It is articulate, erudite, poetic and passionate. Unsurprisingly, he's won numerous awards for his sterling work, and written several books to boot. He is into his eighties now and his writing is as engaging as it ever has been. Over the years, I'm sure John Gibson has had many opportunities to fly the nest for the bright lights of national newspaper offices in London. That he chose to stay and report on his beloved Newcastle United, has enriched the reading pleasure for many thousands of fans in the city. It will be a sad day when I read *The Chronicle* and the writing of John Gibson is no longer on the page. He is a master of his craft.

'Are ye not the trainer for N'castle, like?'

Newcastle United fans are fanatical. They love their football club with an unbridled passion. I think it's fair to say the whole world knows that. I've experienced that devotion since I was 16 years old. The Geordies' love for their club is all-embracing and all-consuming. I have many memories of witnessing it first-hand, but one instance stands out above all others for sheer ridiculousness. The 2005/2006 season was no longer simply about football for me. I was studying law alongside my physiotherapy duties at the club, preparing my exit from professional football for good. I was due to commence bar school at the end of the campaign.

In the weeks leading up to my departure from the club, I took a short break so that I could discreetly shadow an experienced barrister for a few days. It was a very alien world I was entering. I hadn't told anyone at the club of my plans. On my first day, I sat nervously in the conference room of the prestigious Trinity Chambers on Newcastle's Quayside. The eminent barrister was about to hold a conference with a client he was defending. The client was accused of some football-related violence and faced a five-year prison term if found guilty. His client entered the wood-panelled room. He was a giant of a man. He was dressed in a pair of jogging bottoms and wore his Newcastle United shirt with pride, despite his belly protruding from underneath it. The barrister introduced me.

'This is Mr Ferris. He is my colleague and is training to be a barrister. You don't mind if he sits in, do you?'

His client shook his head and shook my hand. He sat across the table as the barrister informed him of the weakness of his defence and the extreme likelihood that he was facing a prison sentence. His best advice in such circumstances might be an early plea of guilty as charged in the hope of some leniency from the judge when it came to sentencing. It was a solemn moment. The barrister was effectively telling the man he was destined to lose his liberty. I felt a little queasy about how I would feel being given such bleak news.

I was still thinking about this when I sensed the client staring intently at me. I was loathe to meet his gaze, but his eyes boring into me left me with little option. He looked at me with a half-smile as he raised his arm to stop his barrister speaking in mid-flow. Then he leaned across the table towards me.

'Here. Excuse me mate, but are yee not the trainer for N'castle, like? Ah knew it was yee like when I first stepped in the room. Clocked it straight away. Ah says to mesel, that's the trainer for N'castle, man.'

He was up on his feet now and walking around the table. There wasn't much else for me to do but rise to meet him and confirm that I was indeed the trainer (physio) for Newcastle United. With that the client completely ignored the fact he was likely going to prison pretty soon. He grabbed my hand between his two and began shaking it furiously.

'Fuck me. Ah fuck'n knew it was yee, like! Fuckin knew, man. Ah thought ah must be gaan mental for a second like. Fuckin mint to meet you an aal that, mate. Fuckin mint.'

It took quite some time to get him back around the table to concentrate on the considerable trouble he was in. If ever you needed evidence of just how fanatical Newcastle fans are, it was there in abundance that day. Can you imagine his reaction if I'd been a player instead of merely the physiotherapist?

I left football shortly afterwards in August 2006, with a fond farewell and a cheque for £7,000 from the generous players. I hugged my friend Ray Thompson, before getting into my car and driving through the gates of the training ground at Darsley Park for the final time. I had to pull the car over before entering the main road because I couldn't see for the tears that flooded my eyes and ran down my cheeks. They came from nowhere and caught me by surprise. I composed myself and told myself not to be so silly and that I was glad to leave it all behind. I truly believed that too. It was, however, still a monumental decision I'd made to leave the comfort and security of the life I'd known for a leap into the complete unknown. It would have been easier to stay, but it was my firm intention to never go back. A life in law lay ahead of me. I was excited for the future.

Then Alan Shearer beckoned. It was easy to say yes to him. So within three years of leaving the club, I abandoned my fledging career as a barrister, and on 1 April, 2009 once again returned to Newcastle United for what would be my third and final time. A foolish decision? The date of my return perhaps provides the answer.

'What will happen to Gareth?'

By far the highlight of my time working as part of Alan Shearer's management team for that brief period at Newcastle United in 2009, was our home game against fellow strugglers Middlesbrough. We were both in the bottom three. Defeat would make survival very difficult for us, while defeat for Middlesborough would all but condemn them to the drop. There was a tense, but raucous, atmosphere inside St James' Park that sunny evening. We went 1-0 down, which only added to the anxiety levels in the stands and on our bench. We equalised, and for a long time it looked like the game was destined for a draw – a result that would be of no help to either team. Alan threw on Obafemi Martins in place of Michael Owen. Within minutes Oba put us in front. With only four minutes remaining, fellow substitute Peter Løvenkrands put the result beyond doubt. We were finally out of the relegation places with two games remaining. Middlesbrough were doomed.

We were naturally very excited in the coaches' room after the game. Euphoric in fact. Then the crestfallen Middlesbrough manager, Gareth Southgate, came in to congratulate Alan Shearer, his former England teammate. The old friends shook hands. There was a palpable warmth between the pair and obviously a lot of mutual respect. Gareth spoke through a wry smile.

'It's easy this management lark. Make a couple of substitutions, win the game and move on.'

The two men spoke for 10 minutes, before the understandably dejected Middlesbrough manager left the room.

We made our way to Alan's house to watch a rerun of the game and have a celebratory glass of wine. My enjoyment of our victory was tempered somewhat by seeing just how crushed the young Middlesbrough manager had been. Alan noticed my mood,

'Crack a smile, man. We won.'

I apologised and spoke about what was troubling me.

'What d'you think will happen to Gareth Southgate?'

Alan confirmed my fears.

'You never know in football, but I think he'll probably lose his job. It's pretty shit sometimes, this game.'

While I felt for Gareth, I was also mightily relieved that night that my future in football looked a lot rosier than his.

The Middlesborough manager did lose his job five months later – which was five months longer than I lasted. I lost mine two weeks after the Middlesbrough game and never worked in football again.

As for Gareth Southgate, whatever did become of him?

'Can I finish my song?'

Newcastle United played Aston Villa away on the final game of the 2008/09 season. The day before the game, we checked in to our hotel in the centre of Birmingham. My room was a very nice but very typical hotel bedroom. I'd barely sat on my bed when I received a call from Alan Shearer.

'Come up and see my room, man, if you want to see how the other half live. You'll see how managers get treated.'

I made my way to the top floor. Alan opened the door and invited me into his suite. It was spectacular. It had its own kitchen, a living room with a grand piano in the corner, and double doors into his bedroom and en-suite. The following morning, I was having breakfast with Nicky Butt. My phone buzzed. It was Alan.

'Can you come up to my room now, please?'

He was flustered, with a panic to his tone I hadn't heard before. I abandoned my breakfast and headed for the elevator. Alan was still in his boxers when he opened the door. I sat on the sofa opposite him. He was rubbing both hands over his forehead.

'Fucking hell, man. You'll never believe what happened to me last night.'

He'd been awakened at 3 a.m. by the sound of music coming from his living room. In a panic, he opened the double doors. There was a couple at the piano. The man was playing it and the woman was draped over it.

'What did you do?' I asked him.

'I fucking shit myself! I shouted at them. I told them to fuck off!'

'Did they fuck off?'

'No. The bloke spoke.'

'What did he say?'

Alan stopped rubbing his head. His panic was replaced by laughter.

'Can I finish my song first?'

I was curious now.

'Did you let him . . . ?'

'Did I fuck! I just kept shouting fuck off until they fucked off. I haven't slept a wink since, man.'

After we'd stopped laughing, I agreed with him that it was indeed a disastrous breach of security. We contacted the hotel management. We watched on CCTV as they showed us the couple entering Alan's room at 2.30 a.m., before scurrying out of it again at 2.55 a.m. They asked Alan if he wanted to take the matter any further. He declined but vowed never to stay in a suite again.

As potentially dangerous as the encounter was for Alan, I still can't help but smile at what the drunk couple must have thought when they were confronted by a terrified Alan Shearer screaming at them to fuck off while dressed in nothing but his underpants!

It was over. I just didn't know it...

Aston Villa away was our date with destiny. Win and we would stay up; draw and we might survive if other results went our way; lose and we would be relegated. We lost.

I've never been in a more dejected changing room than the away changing room at Villa Park that day. We were devastated. Alan stood in the middle of the room and made an impassioned speech about just what Newcastle United meant to him and to the fans in the city. It was brilliant, moving, straight from the heart. It was a glimpse of what kind of leader he would be moving forwards. He spoke about how embarrassing it was for a group of players of such quality to be relegated. He talked about the proud history of the club they had let down, and how sorry he was that we were unable to get the results we needed in the last eight games to keep us up. He was heartbroken for the fans, some of whom he'd known personally since childhood, who'd made the journey to Villa Park full of hope, only to witness capitulation. He spoke of the thousands of fans back in Newcastle, of how they would be feeling tonight, having watched their team slip out of the League without so much as a fight. He finished by telling the players that they should be hurting in a way they never had before in football and, if they weren't hurting, then they shouldn't be at Newcastle United. He intended, he said, to be here next season – and if he was, then some of them certainly wouldn't be.

Alan delivered his lines perfectly. He was calm, articulate, blunt and truthful. I looked around the room. Most players hung on his every word, and some were tearful, clearly devastated. Alan left us there to go and conduct the most difficult press conference of his illustrious career.

Two days after the game, we met with the owner, Mike Ashley. We engaged in serious talks about becoming the permanent management team for the next three years, Alan and Mike then had a private conversation in the manager's office. After the meetings, I drove through

IT WAS OVER. I JUST DIDN'T KNOW IT...

Relegated. No words necessary.

the gates of the training ground, excited for the following season and what I hoped would be the beginning of my next chapter at Newcastle United. It promised to be the best one yet. I remain convinced it would have been. Unfortunately, we never heard from Mike Ashley again.

My 18-year adventure with Newcastle United ended that day – 26 May, 2009. It was over, I just didn't know it. I'm grateful I didn't know. It would have been too much to bear.

A final pilgrimage

I'm no longer a regular at St James' Park. I was one, for quite some time, after leaving in 2009. As the years have passed, and I've suffered some bouts of ill health, priorities have changed. Time spent with my family has become more important. Nothing, not even Newcastle United, gets in the way of a Saturday afternoon with my wife, children and my precious granddaughter, Isla. Having said that, the TV or radio is usually tuned into the match on those days. Old habits die hard.

When Newcastle United is in you, it is in you for life. My brother-in-law, Kieran Moran, is proof positive of that irrefutable truth. He was the man who regaled me with stories of his Geordie heroes back in 1976, even though he'd never visited St James' Park. That all changed for Kieran when I signed as a player and worked as a physiotherapist for the club. Kieran, from never having set foot in Newcastle before, became a regular devotee at St James'. More than that, he had an Access All Areas pass to his football team and the idols who played for it. In the '90s, Kieran was a regular on nights out with the staff and players. He became a familiar face, and was on first name terms with many. One of his prized possessions was a photograph taken at our team hotel on the night of our Cup final defeat to Manchester United, in 1999. In it, he is hugging Alan Shearer, the hero he got to know as a friend. It was the thrill of his life. Kieran was diagnosed with advanced prostate cancer in 2010, and took the devasting news with good grace, as he did with everything else in life. He let the doctors do their thing and got on with enjoying his life.

At Christmas 2022, when it was becoming obvious the disease was starting to wreak havoc, his kids bought him a special Christmas present. They paid for a trip for Kieran and my sister Denise to visit us in Newcastle. More importantly, the trip included two tickets for the Newcastle match against Liverpool. He asked if I would go with him to the match. I realised the moment he did so, that in all the

At the match. Fans take their seats in the stands prior to kick off.

times he had visited St James' before, I had never gone to the match with him. I had always been inside the changing room, working. I hadn't been to a match with Kieran since he took me to Windsor Park in Belfast to watch Northern Ireland play when I was boy. So, it was with considerable excitement that we embarked on the train from Wylam in February 2023, wrapped in our warm coats and black and white scarfs. A pint in The Forth was followed by another in Tilleys. We joined the steady stream of black and white on the short walk up the hill. My heart skipped a little, as it always does, when the huge stands of St James' Park came into view.

The steady stream became a river of black and white as we neared the ground, and when we walked through the tunnel that separated the old and new Milburn reception areas, the stream of black and white became a raging torrent of bodies, chanting and singing. The atmosphere was more intoxicating than the alcohol we'd consumed. Just before kick-off, we took our seats in the Leazes Stand. The whole stadium was rumbling with anticipation of what was to come. The teams took to the pitch. The first bars of Mark Knopfler's 'Going Home: Theme of the Local Hero' rang out. We were on our feet. We hugged. The music stopped, and we added our voices to the almighty roar that erupted from every corner of the stadium. It was electricity. A monumental day.

Then the game started, Liverpool scored twice, and Nick Pope, the Newcastle goalkeeper, was sent off. The game was over as a contest from the 22nd minute. With only injury time remaining, we decided to leave to beat the rush. I walked in front of Kieran. I made my way down the stairs from the stand. I turned, but Kieran was no longer following. I looked back up the stairs. He was standing alone, facing away from me. He was a silhouette, framed in the bright lights of St James' Park. His head moved slowly from side to side, as he stared into the light of the arena. He knew it was his last time. He was a worshipper paying his last respects. He was a lifelong fan, committing the sights and sounds of his beloved St James' Park to memory.

That day, in February 2023, was indeed his last day at the stadium. His health deteriorated rapidly after that. Just over a year later, my sister Elizabeth called to say we needed to go to Ireland immediately, because he was fading faster than anticipated. We booked the first flight we could. We arrived that evening at Kieran and Denise's familiar

The Cathedral roof of St James' Park.

home in Lisburn. Denise, and her adult children, were congregated in the kitchen. No words were necessary. I made my way into the living room with Geraldine. Kieran lay in a hospital bed in front of a giant TV. Fittingly, the football was on. He loved football, though he was oblivious to it now. We sat in silence, not sure if he was even aware of our presence. I put on some music. I played the songs we'd listened to together many times over the years. He'd introduced me to most of the artists. Still there was nothing. Then the first bars of 'Going Home' came on. His hand twitched, his eyes flickered and he half-smiled. Newcastle United was stirring something inside him once more. As the song played, I looked behind his head towards the hallway. There hung his prized possession: the photograph of Kieran embracing Alan Shearer, after the Cup final in 1999. Newcastle United meant the world to him. He lasted only a matter of hours after that.

The Toon Army lost a loyal foot soldier the day Kieran Moran passed away. A family lost an amazing husband and father. I lost a brother-in-law – and, in truth, much more than that.

On Sunday March 16, 2025, Newcastle United beat Liverpool to win The League Cup. A day none of us will ever forget. They did so, 49 years after Dennis Tueart broke Kieran Moran's heart in the final of the same competition in 1976. After 70 long years Newcastle United are domestic trophy winners once more. Sadly Kieran just couldn't hang on long enough to see it. But his Newcastle United fanatic son Kieran did, and so did his son's Dylan and Connor. All three dressed in their Newcastle United shirts visited Kieran's grave in Lisburn before the kick off. Afterwards when the Geordie nation at Wembley, those in Newcastle, and across the world, wildly celebrated the win, 16-year-old Connor Moran slipped unnoticed out of his family home. Still wearing his Newcastle shirt, he walked the short distance to the graveside of his grandfather Kieran. There he sat on a bench in the quiet darkness and told his Granda about Dan Burn, Alexander Isak, Bruno Guimaraes and all the rest. 'We did it Granda. We did it.'

R.I.P Kieran. We did it.

ONCE UPON A TOON

'Run for Home'

I may have departed Newcastle United for the final time 16 years ago, but I've never left the city since my arrival, in 1981. I was in the car this morning and 'Run for Home' came on. It's no real surprise that a song released in 1978 should come on in my car. There's nothing on my Spotify playlist that was released this side of the millennium. It's an age thing. I was a 12-year-old boy growing up in Ireland when I first heard 'Run for Home' on the radio. I had no idea who Lindisfarne were, or where they came from. I didn't care. I just fell in love with the song and the sentiment. The sentiment I felt when I heard it was for the place of my birth, the loving family who reared me, and the familiar streets that I ran around. The song spoke to my sense of belonging. It spoke of Ireland.

When I'd just turned 16 and fate took me away from my home, I found myself living in this strange city of Newcastle, an outpost on the north-east coast of England. If this was the home of Lindisfarne, then I was a reluctant pilgrim. When I heard 'Run for Home' in those early days living in the city that inspired it, the song just made me long even more for the people, the town and the country that I'd left behind.

It's 44 years since I left my home to make a new one here. I still belong to the old one. I always will. But I belong equally as much to this one. The one I learned to live and love in. This is the place where I grew from a shy boy to a husband, a father, and now a grandfather. The people and the place itself just seeped into my bones. Newcastle is now as much a part of me as my childhood home. It is a welcoming, magical place, whose people laugh, hug and sing their way into your heart and then never leave. I'm proud to call my children Geordies. I'm proud to be an adopted Geordie.

I often listen to 'Run for Home'. It's one of my all-time favourite songs. Now when I listen, I don't just think of Ireland. I think of this place. This unique city and its warm people. I think of home. The home I made here a lifetime ago.

Once upon a toon...

Once upon a time there was a great old football team from the north of the kingdom. They played in a mystical place on the hill in the enchanting city of Newcastle. After much early success, the team failed to win a trophy for over half a century. Some said it was cursed. They were just daft bastards, though.

The team did win a trophy once more. Then it won another, and another, and another. There was much singing, dancing and making merry.

... and they all lived happily ever after.

Acknowledgements

I would like to thank my wife Geraldine for her love and support, and her endless patience while having to read, re-read and re-read the manuscript. I must also thank Ed Waugh for the coffee, encouragement and gentle persuasion. Thank you to Alan Shearer for his valued friendship and (yet another) foreword. Thanks also to Michael Walker for his support. And to my agent, Guy Rose, a thank you for your continued efforts to find a home for my writing.

I am extremely grateful for the unwavering support and guidance provided by my editor, Matt Lowing. His belief in my writing means more than he knows. It has been an absolute pleasure to be guided on this journey by him. Thank you to Rachel Nicholson for ensuring my book reaches as many readers as it possibly can and to all at Bloomsbury who have worked on the book in any way, a sincere thank you.

I must acknowledge my boys, Conor, Owen and Ciaran, who fill me with love and pride, and have brought the greatest joy to my life. My final thank you is to my granddaughter Isla. This is another one for you to read when you are a little older. When you do, I want you to know that you were the inspiration for all my writing. See you at the far post.

Love,

Granda x

ACKNOWLEDGEMENTS

St James' Park at night. Noise all around. No better sight. No better sound.

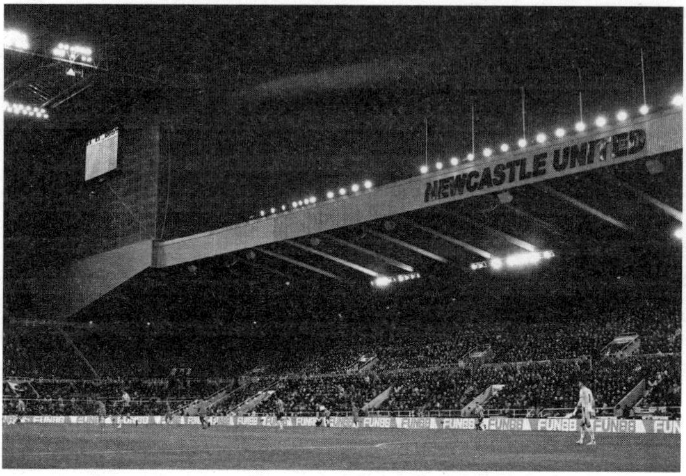
NEWCASTLE UNITED
FUN88